The Classical Origins of Western Culture

The Classical Origins of Western Culture

Core Studies 1

by Roger Dunkle
Department of Classics

Brooklyn College Core Curriculum Series

Brooklyn College Press
Brooklyn, New York

Acknowledgments

I gratefully acknowledge my indebtedness to my colleagues in the Brooklyn College Classics Department, who patiently put up with my early tentative starts at this project and who used those experimental versions with their classes. Their advice and constructive criticisms time and again pointed me in the right direction in matters of format, interpretation, and style. I also owe a debt of gratitude to the editors of the Brooklyn College Press for their careful proofreading and sensible suggestions. My special thanks to my wife, Dr. Ruth Passweg, who supported and encouraged me in this project and whose advice and proofreading were an invaluable aid. I alone take responsibility for whatever errors remain.

July, 1986   Roger Dunkle

Cover illustrations reprinted with permission of the Metropolitan Museum of Art, New York.

Photographs of Greek coins, by Max Hirmer, reprinted with permission of Hirmer Verlag, Munich. Coins are shown approximately four times original size.

ISBN 0–930888–32–4
Library of Congress Catalog Card Number 86–70821

Brooklyn College Press, Brooklyn, New York 11210
© 1986 by Brooklyn College, The City University of New York
All rights reserved. Published 1986.

Printed in the United States of America
Designed by Strong Cohen

Contents

Preface

The concept of this study guide to Core Studies 1, "The Classical Origins of Western Culture," exemplifies both the creativity of the ten-course Core Curriculum that is now part of the education of every Brooklyn College student and the additional creativity the Core has stimulated in the Brooklyn College faculty. I would like to pay special tribute to the members of the Classics Department who developed the innovative approach of this book. I would also like to recognize the contributions of the Core Editorial Committee.

Although Core Studies 1 deals specifically with the *classical* origins of Western culture, we are all well aware that Western civilization developed not solely on the basis of the Greco-Roman experience, but also on the basis of Judeo-Christian and extra-European history and traditions. Nevertheless, without an understanding of the Greco-Roman contribution, we would not have the foundaiton to enable us to understand fully Western literature, legal systems, or institutions. More than one thousand years passed between the fall of the Roman Empire and the Enlightenment, but clearly the links between the classical and the neoclassical are real, and understanding of those links is indispensable.

The words of Horace live today in the motto inscribed on the Brooklyn College Seal, "Nil sine magno labore" ("Nothing without great effort"). Core Studies 1 is a difficult course but, we believe, worth the effort.

Robert L. Hess
President
Brooklyn College

Introduction

This study guide was written to help students read and interpret the ancient texts assigned in Core Studies 1 "The Classical Origins of Western Culture," the first of ten required courses in Brooklyn College's Core Curriculum. Because it is among the first core courses taken by students upon entering Brooklyn College, this course obviously bears a special responsibility for laying a firm groundwork for students' future core studies. When this course was first taught in 1981, it became immediately clear that students needed assistance in dealing with sophisticated literary texts. The many available review books that are so popular with students do not solve, but actually contribute to, the problem. These books present summaries of literary works that encourage the students to avoid grappling with the literary text; in fact, some students read the summary rather than the work itself. Therefore, this study guide was designed to focus attention on the literature by posing questions in the "Exercises for Reading Comprehension and Interpretation" that are keyed to the selections read in Core Studies 1 and that lead the student step by step through the reading. Some of the more inferential questions could also be used as a springboard for classroom discussion, but they are in no way intended to replace questions devised by individual teachers that reflect their special interests and approaches. The main purpose of the exercises is to provide a kind of checklist to help students better comprehend their reading assignments.

Although the questions are the soul of this study guide, there is other material that can serve a useful purpose in Core Studies 1. The supplemental information provided in each unit and the background narratives (for example, "Philosophical Background of the Fifth Century B.C.") are intended to make it less necessary for the teacher to lecture and thus free more class time for concentration on the assigned texts. In addition, at the end of the guide there is a section on writing a Core Studies 1 paper, a chronological table, and a glossary.

How to Use the Study Guide for Core Studies 1

The "Exercises for Reading Comprehension and Interpretation" form the most important part of the study guide. One of the aims of Core Studies 1 is to teach you to read literary texts with understanding. The questions contained in these exercises are designed to focus your attention on the literary texts by leading you step by step through them. A good method would be to read a portion of the assignment and then stop to see if you can answer the relevant questions in the exercises. Continue with this procedure to the end of the assignment. You might be able to answer some questions easily; others might be more difficult. Some might stump you completely, but in that case you should ask your instructor about them. This process requires a fair amount of effort, but it is very valuable for learning and much more profitable than using the plot summaries given in review books. If you feel you must use review books, be sure never to use them as a substitute for the assigned text. Reading a plot summary of a literary work is not the same as reading the work itself.

In addition to the exercises, this guide provides a considerable amount of supplemental information intended to enrich your understanding of the literary texts. For example, in the unit on the Iliad, preceding the exercise on Book 1,[1] there are sections on genre, reading the *Iliad*, the heroic code, and the gods. These could be read either before or after doing the exercise. The best practice would be to read them before doing the exercise and then again afterward. The first reading of these sections would put you on the alert for significant ideas in the text, and the second reading would be even more meaningful because of your acquaintance with the text. The background narratives that are not part of a unit on a literary work (for example, "Philosophical Background of the Fifth Century B.C.") should be read in conjunction with the study of whatever work immediately follows it in the guide, unless you are told otherwise by your instructor.

Be sure also to take advantage of the sections at the end of this guide: Writing a Core Studies 1 Paper, Chronological Table, and Glossary. The last two are especially valuable when reviewing for an exam. The Chronological Table can help you put the literary works you have read into a historical framework. The Glossary is a handy alphabetical listing that includes not only important terms with their definitions, but also significant characters, events, and places with their identifications. Finally, you should consult the maps of Greece and of Rome for the location of important places.

[1] The Greeks and Romans called divisions of literary works books.

- Epidamnus

M A C E D O N I A

Potidaea •

A E G E A N

Corcyra

Actium •

Thermopylae •

Delphi •

Thebes •

•Marath

•Athens

Corinth •

Mycenae •

Salamis

(Mykenai) • Argos

Olympia •

P E L O P O N N E S U S

I O N I A N

• Lacedaemonia (Sparta)

S E A

Melo

Ancient Greece

• Troy (Ilion)

S E A

Lesbos   • Mytilene

Chios

$I O N I A$

Samos

Miletus •

◄ Delos

Rhodes

ete

Homer, the Greek epic poet, author
of the *Iliad* and the *Odyssey*.
Ios, c. 325–300 B.C.

Iliad
Homer

Genre: Epic

Literary works are classified according to various categories called genres, each having their own characteristic form and content. The *Iliad*[1] belongs to the genre of epic. An epic is a long poem that tells a story involving gods, heroes, and heroic exploits. Since the epic is by its very nature lengthy, it tends to be rather loosely organized. Not every episode is absolutely necessary to the main story, and digressions are not uncommon. You will notice how different in this regard is the genre of drama, in which every episode tends to be essential to the plot and digressions are inappropriate. The events narrated in epic are drawn from legend, rather than invented by the poet, and are typically of great significance. Such is the case with the *Iliad*, which relates an important incident centering around the greatest hero of the Greeks in the Trojan War, the most celebrated war of Greek legend. The epic poet tends to present his narrative impersonally, not drawing attention to himself except occasionally, as in the first line of the *Iliad* when Homer addresses the goddess who is the Muse[2] of epic poetry.

Reading the Iliad

When you first read the *Iliad*, the beginning of the poem can present some difficulty because it assumes a general familiarity with the war between the Trojans and Greeks that most modern readers, unlike the ancient Greeks, do not possess. You should have no trouble, however, if you keep a few facts in mind. The war had been occasioned by an offense given twenty years earlier to Menelaos, the Greek king of Sparta, by the Trojan prince, Paris (also called Alexandros). Paris, aided by the goddess Aphrodite, whom he had judged the winner of a beauty contest over the goddesses Athene and Hera, had stolen Menelaos's wife, Helen. In order to recover Helen, Menelaos's brother, Agamemnon, the powerful king of Mykenai, had gathered together a large force that included many prominent Greek warriors, themselves either princes or kings. The greatest of these was the hero, Achilleus, the central character of the *Iliad*. The main story of the poem consists of the experiences of Achilleus within a rather limited period of time (fifty-four days) in the tenth year of the war.

---

[1] The word *Iliad* means "a poem about Ilion [another name for Troy]."
[2] In Greek myth a Muse is one of the nine daughters of Zeus, who are goddesses of the arts. See line 604 of the first book of the *Iliad*.

Another problem you might encounter in your first reading of the poem is the language in which the story is told. After reading even a small portion of the *Iliad*, one quickly becomes aware of Homer's distinctive style, which is characterized by the constant repetition of phrases, whole lines, and even whole passages. The name *Achilleus* is frequently accompanied by the phrase "of the swift feet."[3] Apollo is often described as he "who strikes from afar." Speeches are repeatedly introduced by such phrases as "Then in answer again spoke. . ." and summed up by "So he spoke." You could no doubt provide numerous other examples of this stylistic phenomenon. What is most unusual about the recurring descriptive words applied to the name of a god or goddess, hero or heroine, or inanimate things is that, although they are sometimes relevant to their context, they most often are irrelevant and, therefore, seemingly unnecessary. For example, it is helpful to the reader to have Agamemnon identified once or twice as "lord of men" and Achilleus called "brilliant" and "of the swift feet," but the frequent repetition of these descriptive words throughout the poem reveals that their purpose goes beyond identification. The description of Apollo in Book 1, line 21, as the one "who strikes from afar," has some relevance because the god will send a destructive plague into the Achaian camp by shooting arrows from his silver bow (1. 48-51).[4] But there are many more of these repeated descriptions that are totally irrelevant. The Achaian ships are often called "fast" when they are not in motion. Odysseus is twice called "crafty" in Book 1 although he engages in no tricks. The sea is referred to as "barren" for no apparent purpose. Even the relevant epithets[5] lose their relevance when they are constantly repeated, as is the case with Apollo, who continues to be referred to as he "who strikes from afar" throughout the rest of Book 1, without any connection with the action. The problem is further complicated by the fact that other epithets are also applied to Apollo, such as "King," "Phoibos," "radiant," "beloved of Zeus," "archer," "who works from afar," and others, with a similar lack of relevance.

The reason for the constant repetitions in the *Iliad* is that Homer composed in an oral style, which involved the improvisation of poetry without

---

[3] All quotations from the *Iliad* are from Richmond Lattimore's translation (Chicago: University of Chicago, 1961).

[4] References to the *Iliad* will be given by the book number (before the period) and line numbers (after the period).

[5] An *epithet* is a descriptive word or phrase that is linked with the name of a person or thing. Remember that you can also consult the Glossary for terms, as well as characters, events, and places.

the aid of writing. In order to facilitate the adaptation of his words to the requirements of the dactylic hexameter, the traditional meter of Greek epic poetry, the oral poet used stock phrases called formulas, which aided him in filling out various metrical portions of the line. A character or object in the *Iliad* generally has a number of epithets of varying metrical size used in conjunction with it. The reason for this is that sometimes a longer epithet is needed to suit the meter, while on other occasions a shorter one is needed. For example, in lines 58, 84, 364, and 489 of Book 1, a metrically longer epithet is required to describe Achilleus; therefore, he is referred to as Achilleus "of the swift feet." But in lines 7 and 292 of the same book, a metrically shorter epithet is needed; so he is called "brilliant."

The term *formula* can also be used in reference to other elements larger than the name plus epithet. A whole line can be formulaic, such as the line that is regularly employed at the end of a meal:

But after they had put away their desire for eating and drinking. . .

Also formulaic are whole passages that are repeated in almost exactly the same language with a closely corresponding sequence of events, as is evident in the description of a sacrifice and a meal in Book 1, lines 458-69 and Book 2, lines 421-32. Messages tend to be repeated or stories retold in almost exactly the same language.

These repetitions are essential to the oral style of composition. They not only aided the poet in composing, but also helped the audience, who did not have the benefit of a text, to remember the details of the story. If these repeated formulas had been merely practical necessities, however, the *Iliad* would not have succeeded as poetry. In addition to their practical purpose, these formulas, with their emphasis on particulars, create an indelibly vivid impression of the characters and the Homeric world in general. Who can forget "swift-footed Achilleus," "fair-cheeked Briseis," "Zeus who gathers the clouds," the "glancing-eyed Achaians," or the "infinite water"? Some formulas paint an especially vivid picture: "Dawn with her rosy fingers," "Hera of the white arms," and "the shadowy mountains and the echoing sea." The formulaic line that is often used to describe the death of a hero has a power that survives its many repetitions:

He fell thunderously and his armor clattered upon him.

You will no doubt find your own favorites in the poem.

Be patient with this oral style of composition; you will soon become used to it. Also, do not be put off by the great variety of characters and actions. The *Iliad* is like a very large painting that contains crowds of people and many insignificant events, but focuses on a central action. These details are not important individually, but do create an impression of largeness and provide an imposing background for the main focus of the painting. Confronted for the first time with a poem with a large cast of characters and the seemingly countless details of the narrative, you might find yourself somewhat confused. But if you read carefully and are willing to reread, you will find that the main story of the *Iliad* is fairly simple and involves a relatively small number of major characters.

Heroic Code

The code that governs the conduct of the Homeric heroes is a simple one. The aim of every hero is to achieve honor, that is, the esteem of one's peers. Honor is essential to the Homeric heroes, so much so that life would be meaningless without it. Thus honor is more important than life itself. As you will notice in reading the *Iliad*, when a hero is advised to avoid a life-threatening situation in battle, his only choice is to ignore this warning. A hero's honor is determined primarily by his courage and physical abilities and to a lesser degree by his social status and possessions. The highest honor can be won only in battle, for here competition is fiercest and the stakes are the greatest. Two other heroic activities, hunting and athletics, could win the hero only an inferior honor. An even lesser honor was won by the sole nonphysical heroic activity, the giving of advice in council (1. 490; 9. 443). Nestor, who is too old to fight, makes a specialty of giving advice, since that is the only heroic activity left to him (1. 254-84).

The heroic ideal in the *Iliad* is sometimes offensive to modern sensibility, but what is required here is not the reader's approval, but understanding of these heroic values. One can understand the *Iliad* only if one realizes what motivates action in the poem. Indeed, Homeric heroism is savage and merciless. Thus the hero often finds himself in a pressure-filled, kill-or-be-killed situation. Success means survival and greater honor; failure means death and elimination from the competition for honor. Victory in battle, however, is not enough in itself; it is ephemeral and can be easily forgotten. The victor, therefore, seeks to acquire a permanent symbol of his victory in the form of the armor of the defeated enemy. As you will notice, furious battles break out over the corpse, as the victor tries to strip the armor and the associates of the defeated warrior try to prevent him. Occasionally prizes from the spoils of war are awarded for valor in battle as in the cases of Chryseis and Briseis, who were given respectively to Agamemnon and Achilleus. The importance of these captive girls as symbols of honor is evident in the dispute that arises in Book 1. The Homeric hero is also fiercely individualistic; he is primarily concerned with his own honor and that of his household,[6] which is only an extension of himself. As is particularly true of Achilleus, the Homeric hero is not likely to be as concerned about his fellow warriors as he is about himself and the members of his household. Loyalty to the community or city (*polis*) had not yet achieved the importance it was going to have in later times.

The Homeric heroes did not enjoy war for its own sake, but viewed it as the best opportunity for the highest honor. In their view, war involves the constant risk of death, which gives meaning to life. This is illustrated in the following speech of Sarpedon (12. 322-28):

> Man, supposing you and I, escaping this battle
> would be able to live on forever, ageless, immortal,
> so neither would I myself go on fighting in the foremost
> nor would I urge you into the fighting where men win glory.
> But now, seeing that the spirits of death stand close about us
> in their thousands, no man can turn aside nor escape them,
> let us go on and win glory for ourselves or yield it to others.

The moral pressure that ensures compliance with this heroic code is simply what peers will think and say. The Homeric hero is supremely concerned with the reaction of his fellow heroes to his actions, since ultimately it is they alone who can bestow honor. When Hektor's wife urges him not to re-enter the war, he answers (6. 441-43):

> . . . yet I would feel deep shame
> before the Trojans, and the Trojan women with trailing garments,
> if like a coward I were to shrink aside from the fighting;

Hektor is not free to walk away from the war. His fear of adverse public opinion forces him to ignore the pleas of his wife and risk his life for the sake of honor. One must fight courageously, whatever the cost. As Odysseus says (11. 408-10):

> . . . I know that it is the cowards who walk out of the fighting,
> but if one is to win honour in battle, he must by all means
> stand his ground strongly, whether he be struck or strike down another.

---

6 The household, or *oikos*, consisted not only of blood relatives, but also of retainers like Phoinix and Patroklos, who enjoy a close relationship with Achilleus.

Achilleus, the hero of Homer's *Iliad.*
Epirus, Pyrrhus, 297-272 B.C.

Gods

The religion of the ancient Greeks was polytheistic[7] and involved the worship of various gods who presided over different aspects of the physical world and human experience: for example, Zeus, god of the sky; Aphrodite, goddess of sex; Ares, god of war. The Greek gods are not spiritual beings, but are anthropomorphic.[8] They resemble human beings and tend to act in a human way, displaying all human emotions, virtues, and vices. Their anthropomorphism is further illustrated by the patriarchal organization of the divine family, which imitates the patriarchy[9] of human society. Zeus is the patriarch of the gods. He demands, but does not always get, the obedience of the other gods. The importance of both divine and human patriarchy in the Homeric world can be seen in the frequent use of patronymics[10] in the *Iliad* (for example, Zeus, son of Kronos; Achilleus, son of Peleus). One of the most important things that can be said about a god or mortal is the identity of the father.

It should be noted that Homer's depiction of the gods in the *Iliad* is more the result of the poet's inventive imagination than a literal representation of the gods of ancient Greek religious observance. Homer is more concerned with making the gods suit the thematic needs of his poem than he is in inspiring religious piety in his audience. It is quite clear that on one level the gods in the *Iliad* act as a foil[11] for humanity by accenting the troubles and sufferings experienced by men in contrast with the joys and general ease of divine existence. For this reason, appearances of the gods in the *Iliad* are sometimes characterized by comedy in order to emphasize human misfortune by contrast. In fact, Herodotus, the fifth-century historian, says that Homer and Hesiod, an epic poet contemporary with Homer, first named the gods, determined their honors and functions, and devised their physical appearance (2. 53).

In the *Iliad* the gods are very much concerned with human affairs. One reason for this involvement is the fact that many gods and goddesses have human children or human favorites participating in the war. The gods take sides in the war in accordance with their like or dislike of one side or the other. For example, Athene and Hera, who lost the beauty contest judged

---

[7] Characterized by the worship of many gods.

[8] Having human characteristics.

[9] Father-rule.

[10] A name inherited from a paternal ancestor.

[11] A person or thing that emphasizes, through contrast, the distinctive traits of another person or thing.

by the Trojan prince Paris, are fiercely anti-Trojan, while the winner, Aphrodite, dotes on Paris and favors the Trojans in the war.

The interest and involvement of the gods in human affairs have an important effect on the action of the *Iliad*. The gods *universalize* the action of the poem. Because the gods take an interest in human affairs, the events described in the *Iliad* are not merely particular actions of little significance, but take on a universal meaning and importance that would have been missing without the gods. Thus, the involvement of the gods exalts human action. For example, when Achilleus, in Book 1, considers killing Agamemnon, his decision not to kill could have been presented on a purely human level without the intervention of a deity, but we are shown, by the involvement of Athene, exactly how critical a decision it is. Throughout the *Iliad* there is a tendency to present action consistently on two planes, the human and the divine. But the gods also serve to emphasize the limitations of man, how short his life is, and, quite paradoxically in view of the previously stated purpose, how ultimately futile human endeavors are.

Book 1: Exercise for Reading Comprehension and Interpretation

First of all, in order to understand the *Iliad* you must try to identify the main theme[12] of the poem. Once identified, the main theme will help you separate the essential action of the *Iliad* from the action that is not crucial to the central plot. The main theme is presented by Homer in the first line of the poem. What is this theme? Here is the first line in Greek followed first by a transliteration and then by a word-for-word translation:

Μῆνιν ἄειδε, Θεά, Πηληιάδεω Ἀχιλῆος

Mēnin aeide, theā, Pēlēiadeō Achilēos

Anger sing of, goddess, of Peleus's son Achilleus

Note the difference between the word order at the beginning of the line and the normal English arrangement. How does the Greek word order help you identify the main theme?

---

[12] A *theme* in literature is a central idea that gives a literary work logical unity.

After the introduction of the poem (1-7), Homer tries to create immediate interest by thrusting his audience *in medias res*, "into the middle of things". This Latin phrase is used in literary criticism to refer to the epic poet's practice of beginning his story without an introduction to the main characters and without an explanation of the situation that forms the background of the story (that is, without any exposition). The first action of the poem is a suppliancy, that is, a ritual act, in which the suppliant, while sitting or kneeling, grasps the knees of the person supplicated and touches his chin or kisses his hands (see 1. 500-1 and 24. 478). This act of self-humiliation was an attempt to forestall any unfavorable reaction on the part of the supplicated. Once the supplication was properly performed, the suppliant was under the protection of Zeus; anyone who rejected a supplication risked the anger of that god. What request does Chryses make of Agamemnon (20)? What is the reaction of the Achaians[13] (22-23)? What is Agamemnon's response (26-32)? Why does Chryses pray to Apollo and what prayer does he make (36-42)? How does Apollo answer his prayer (43-52)?

What advice does Achilleus give to Agamemnon in the midst of the plague (59-67)? What does Kalchas fear (74-83)? What effect is Achilleus's assurance of protection to Kalchas (85-91) likely to have on Agamemnon? What explanation does Kalchas give of the plague (93-100)? What is Agamemnon's reaction (106-20)? Why does Achilleus say that Agamemnon should not demand an immediate replacement for Chryseis (122-29)? What is Agamemnon's answer to Achilleus (131-39)? Why does Achilleus take Agamemnon's vague threat so personally (149-71)? What specific threat does Agamemnon make to Achilleus (181-87)? What is Achilleus's reaction to this threat (188-94), and what is the result of Athene's intervention (216-21)? What is the meaning of Achilleus's dashing the sceptre to the ground (233-46)? What is the purpose of Nestor's speech (254-84)? What are the reactions of Agamemnon and Achilleus to this speech (286-303)?

What is Achilleus's conduct toward the heralds of Agamemnon who come to get Briseis (334-44)? What important fact do we find out about Achilleus when he calls to his mother (352-56)? What request does Achilleus ask Thetis to make of Zeus (407-12)?

What is the purpose of the prayer and sacrifice that Chryses makes to Apollo in lines 451-74?

---

[13] Homer uses three names, with no apparent difference in meaning, to refer to the people whom we call Greeks: *Achaians*, *Danaans*, and *Argives*.

Describe the feelings of Achilleus after his decision to withdraw from the war (488-92). What request does Thetis make of Zeus (505-10)? What is Zeus's answer, and why is he disturbed by the request (518-27)? What complaint does Hera make to Zeus (540-43)? Why is she disturbed by Thetis's supplication of Zeus (555-59)? What is Zeus's reaction to her complaints (545-50; 561-67)? What is Hephaistos's advice to Hera (573-83)? Why do the gods laugh (599-600)? In Book 1, how do the events on Mt. Olympus reflect events on earth? Compare the result of the quarrel between Achilleus and Agamemnon and that between Zeus and Hera. What is the main difference between the quality of human and divine life?

Character Analysis

First, you should note that the word character is used in literary criticism in two different ways. It can mean a personage in a literary work (for example, Achilleus, in the *Iliad*) or the personal traits that make such a personage a well-defined individual (Achilleus's tendency to anger and his other distinctive characteristics). The term *character analysis* refers to the examination of a character's personal traits.

When you attempt a character analysis, there are several things that you must take into consideration. The personality of any character is revealed in what the character says, thinks, and does, and what other characters and the author in his own person say about that character. Although the evaluation of the personality of a character is most important in a character analysis, you should not neglect physical appearance and condition, which also can have an important effect on character and action (for example, Helen's beauty and Nestor's and Priam's old age).

Book 3 is especially rich in characterization, particularly in reference to the two people whose actions were the cause of the war—Paris and Helen. Paris's character is revealed not only by his words and actions, but also by implicit contrast with his brother, Hektor. Helen is presented as a complex character, who realizes the wrong she has done and who despises Paris, but yet seems unable to give up her sexual relationship with him. The analysis of her ambivalent character is further complicated by the control that Aphrodite exercises over her. One general rule, however, should be kept in mind with regard to divine influence on human behavior. The gods tend to influence characters to act in a way consistent with their own personalities. For example, the close relationship of Aphrodite, the goddess of sexual love, with Paris and Helen, is probably an indication that sexual desire is a predominant drive in their psychological make-up. Conversely, Aphrodite never exerts an influence on Hektor, whose personality makes him primarily a fighter rather than a lover.

As you read the *Iliad*, make note of the evidence in the text that gives insight into the personalities of important characters. The better you understand the characters of the *Iliad*, the better you will understand their actions. One note of warning: characters in a literary work are not real human beings, but have been created by the author to suit the needs of the story. Always keep this in mind in character analysis.

Irony

Irony is a frequently used device in literature and may be employed in various ways. One kind of irony is evident when literary characters, in word or deed, make assumptions that the reader or audience know to be false or make statements of which the characters cannot know the significance until later in the work. This kind of irony is often referred to as "dramatic irony" because of its frequent use in drama, but this term is also loosely applied to the same phenomenon in narrative works like the *Iliad*. Dramatic irony underlines the frustration suffered by central characters in literature in the pursuit of their own happiness. A classic example of dramatic irony occurs in Sophocles' play *Oedipus the King*, in which the hero Oedipus curses the killer of his predecessor in the kingship, not knowing that he himself is the murderer. Watch out for examples of dramatic irony in the *Iliad*; they are important for a proper understanding of the poem.

Simile and Metaphor

A simile is a comparison of two unlike things introduced by *like* or *as*. For example, Menelaos is compared to a wild beast because of his eagerness to find Paris, who had been rescued by Aphrodite: "Menelaos was wandering through the throng *like a wild beast. . .*" (3. 449). The basic purpose of this or any simile is to present a word-picture that will make the reader experience in a more vivid way what is being described. In the above example Menelaos's movement in search of Paris is brought to life by the picture of a wild beast, which suggests the frantic agitation of a man who has been frustrated in his desire for revenge. The simile is an important feature of Homer's style. He uses both short similes like the one above and extended ones that became a standard feature of the epic tradition after Homer. The first thirty-five lines of Book 3 contain four extended similes.

Akin to the simile is a figure of speech called a metaphor, a comparison between two different things without the use of *like* or *as*. The simile describing Menelaos stated that he was like a wild beast. That simile could be stated as a metaphor: "Menelaos is a wild beast." This, of course, does not mean that Menelaos is literally a wild beast, but that at this time he shares some characteristics with a wild beast. Metaphors are not as common in the *Iliad* as similes, but they do occur as in the formulaic phrase "winged words" (1. 201). Obviously, words do not have wings, birds do. But words do fly out of the mouth like birds, and once they have been said, they are as hard to take back as birds are to capture.

Book 3: Exercise

What contrast is suggested by the description of the Trojans and the Achaians in lines 1-9? by the description of Menelaos and Alexandros (Paris) in lines 15-37? Why is Hektor upset by Paris's behavior (38-57)? What difference does Paris see between himself and Hektor (59-66)? What proposal does Paris make (67-75)? What is Helen doing when she first appears in the narrative (125-27)? What is the symbolic significance of her action? Why is Helen summoned by Iris (130-38)? How does Homer depict Helen's beauty (156-60)? What does Helen do for Priam (161-242)? Do you find anything strange in the questions asked of Helen by Priam at this point in the war (the tenth year)? What purpose does the information given by Helen serve in the *Iliad*? What literary device is Homer employing in lines 236-44?

What are the terms of the duel (281-91)? What crime of Paris does Menelaos mention in his prayer to Zeus (351-54)? What does Aphrodite's intervention prevent (373-82)? Why does Aphrodite want Helen to go to Paris's chamber (390-94)? What is Helen's reaction to the goddess's invitation (399-412)? What threat does Aphrodite make to Helen (414-17)? What criticism does Helen make of Paris (428-36)? What is Paris's reaction to this criticism (438-46)? Helen's actions in this scene are obviously inconsistent with her feelings. What is the reason for her inconsistency?

What purpose does Book 3 serve? Does it advance the story begun in Book 1 at all? Explain your answer.

Foreshadowing

Homer often gives his audience hints about what is going to happen later in the story. This technique is called *foreshadowing* and conveys a sense of the inevitability of important events. An example of foreshadowing occurs in Book 6 when Hektor leaves Andromache to return to battle while her handmaidens mourn for him as if he were already dead (500-2). Note also Hektor's pessimism, which he expresses to Andromache (447-65). This foreshadowing prepares us for Hektor's death in Book 22. Achilleus's approaching death (which does not occur in the *Iliad*) is also foreshadowed, as early as Book 1, by himself and his mother (352; 416).

The above examples are only the most obvious instances of foreshadowing in the *Iliad*. Try to find other more subtle instances of anticipation of future events.

Book 6: Exercise

Book 6 begins with the deaths of minor figures on the Trojan side, many of whom Homer brings briefly to life with a few words before they are killed. What is the intended effect of Homer's description of Axylos (12-15)? Evaluate the words and actions of Agamemnon in the case of Adrestos in the light of Homeric morality (44-60).

What order does Helenos give to Hektor (86-95)? What is unusual about this order? Why does Diomedes, the son of Tydeus, ask Glaukos to identify himself (123-43)? What comment does Glaukos's simile in lines 146-50 make on humanity? The story that Glaukos tells about his grandfather, Bellerophontes, has little or no connection with the plot, but has an interest of its own as a heroic tale. The typically loose organization of the epic form easily accommodates such a digression, which would be intolerable in a smaller and more tightly structured form like drama. What discovery does Diomedes make when Glaukos mentions his grandfather (215-31)? What is the result of Diomedes' discovery (232-36)?

After he delivers Helenos's message to his mother, Hekabe, what does Hektor tell her he intends to do (280)? What is Hektor's attitude toward Paris (281-85)? What is Athene's reaction to the prayers and gift of the Trojan women (311)? What literary device is Homer employing here? Explain your answer.

What does Hektor encourage Paris to do (326-31)? How does Paris react to Hektor's words (333-41)? What is Helen's view of herself and Paris (343-53)? Where does Hektor go next (365)? What does Andromache fear (405-10)? Note carefully Andromache's story about the death of her father at the hands of Achilleus (414-28). It is a foreshadowing of Achilleus's behavior in the last book of the *Iliad*. What does Andromache think is most notable about Achilleus's conduct with regard to her father? What request does Andromache make of Hektor (431-34)? In Hektor's mind what prevents him from doing what his wife asks (440-46)? What does Hektor foresee for the Trojans and his wife (447-65)? In the context of this sorrow-filled situation (466-71), what is the intended effect of the laughter of Hektor and Andromache at their son's terror? What hopes does Hektor have for his son (476-81)? What literary device is evident in this expression of Hektor's hopes? What is Hektor's state of mind as he leaves his family (486-93)? What literary device is evident in line 500? What do we learn about Hektor's character from his meetings with Hekabe, Paris, Helen, and Andromache?

What comment does the simile in lines 506-11 make on the character of Paris? What are Hektor's feelings about Paris (521-25)?

What purpose does Book 6 serve? Does it advance the story begun in Book 1 at all? Explain your answer.

Book 9: Exercise

How are the Achaians doing in the war at this point in the story (1-8)? Note the capitalization of the first letters of *Panic* and *Terror* in line 2 (see *Hate* in Book 11, line 4). The reason for this is that these two human emotions are personified as minor divinities by Homer. What recommendation does Agamemnon make to the Achaians (17-28)? What criticism does Diomedes make of Agamemnon (38-39)? What is Diomedes' attitude with regard to the war (45-49)? What advice does Nestor give to Agamemnon (96-113)? How does Agamemnon react to this advice (115-61)? Which Achaians does Nestor suggest should go to Achilleus (168-70)? Why doesn't Agamemnon go himself?

What is Achilleus doing when these men arrive at his hut (186-89)? How does Achilleus behave toward them (197-204)? What is Patroklos's role in this scene (201-20)? Then, each ambassador delivers a speech, which is in turn answered by Achilleus. You no doubt have noted that Homer frequently employs speeches in his narrative. Throughout ancient times speech-making was the primary means of mass communication. Writing did exist, but without a printing press, publication of written material was very limited. Thus, it is natural that speeches are prominent in the *Iliad*. The speeches also give a lively dramatic quality to the poem. This quality often leads students to make the mistake of calling the *Iliad* a play—a dramatic performance in which actors impersonate characters—when it is really a narrative poem—a genre in which a storyteller or narrator relates the whole story. Odysseus is spokesman for Agamemnon and therefore speaks first because of his rhetorical skills (see 3. 216-23). Although Odysseus repeats word for word most of Agamemnon's earlier speech (115-61), he makes purposeful additions and omissions. Read Odysseus's speech (225-306) carefully and identify these additions and omissions. Explain the reason for each addition and omission.

To whom do you think Achilleus is referring in lines 312-13? Achilleus then presents his reasons for rejecting Agamemnon's offer (315-420). Briefly summarize these reasons. Do you find them convincing? Explain your answer. What does Achilleus say he will do now that he has refused to accept the gifts (357-63; 426-29)?

The speech of Phoinix is divided into three sections: Phoinix's relationships with his own father, with Achilleus's father (Peleus), and with Achilleus (447-95); the parable of the Prayers (502-12); and the example of Meleagros (529-99). What effect does Phoinix hope lines 485-96 will have on Achilleus? What is Phoinix's basic message to Achilleus (496-501)? Phoinix's story of the spirits of Prayer is a *parable*—a story illustrating a moral lesson. In this story, what we would regard as psychological phenomena internal to a human being are personified as minor divinities. Ruin represents the tendency to give offense to others. The spirits of Prayer represent the desire to make amends by asking forgiveness. What point does this parable make? The story of Meleagros is an instance of the technique commonly used by Homeric characters of giving a mythological example to make an argument more persuasive. Although this story is long and detailed, its essential message is clear and simple. What is this message (600-5)? What is Achilleus's response to Phoinix's speech (607-19)?

What is the main point of Aias's brief speech (624-42)? What is Achilleus's response to this speech (644-55)? What does Odysseus report to Agamemnon (677-92)? Is Odysseus's report entirely accurate? Explain your answer. What is Diomedes' reaction to this report (697-709)?

Describe Achilleus's state of mind in Book 9. Does he really believe everything he says to Odysseus? Explain your answer.

Book 11: Exercise

What purpose does the wounding of Agamemnon, Diomedes, Odysseus, and Eurypylos serve at this point in the story (1-590)? What significance do the disasters suffered by the Achaians have for Achilleus (608-9)? What do lines 598-614 say about Achilleus's feelings with regard to the war and the Achaians? What literary device is evident in line 603? What order does Achilleus give to Patroklos (610-14)?

How is Nestor's speech (655-802; compare 1. 254-84) typical of him? What suggestion does Nestor make to Patroklos (791-802)? What do you think is the effect of Eurypylos's words (822-35) on Patroklos?

Book 16: Exercise

Why does Patroklos mention the wounding of the Achaian chieftains to Achilleus (23-29)? Explain the meaning of the metaphors of the sea and rocks in lines 34-35. What request does Patroklos make of Achilleus, and what does he hope to accomplish, if Achilleus consents (38-45)? Read lines 49-63 carefully. Explain why Achilleus agrees to Patroklos's request. What warning does Achilleus give to Patroklos (87-96)? Why does Achilleus give this warning? What frustration does Achilleus's prayer to the gods reveal (97-100)?

What emergency critical to the fortunes of the Achaians arises (112-24)? After the formulaic scene of Patroklos's arming (130-44), Achilleus prepares his men, the Myrmidons, for battle. Homer then presents a catalogue of the Myrmidons (168-97). Catalogue poetry is an important feature of the epic. In Book 2 there is an elaborate catalogue of the Achaians at Troy and a smaller one of the Trojans. In Book 18 there is also a catalogue of the daughters of Nereus, who are mourning the death of Patroklos (39-49). What comment do the similes in lines 156-63 and 259-65 make on the character of the Myrmidons? What was their attitude with regard to Achilleus's withdrawal from the war (200-9)? What prayer does Achilleus make to Zeus (241-48)? What literary device is evident in lines 249-52?

Fate in the *Iliad* is not a force that predetermines *all* human actions. Fate refers primarily to ends, like the end of a man's life or of a city, such as Troy. These ends are governed by fate and cannot be avoided. The relationship of the gods to fate is an issue in the conversation between Zeus and Hera. What action does Zeus consider in lines 435-38? What warning does Hera give to Zeus (440-49)? Is fate the same as the will of the gods? What control do the gods have over fate? What does Zeus's sorrow for Sarpedon's death add to the account of his son's death (459-61)?

What is Patroklos's first concern after killing Sarpedon (558-61)? What is the effect of the extended simile describing the battle over Sarpedon's armor (641-43)? What request does Zeus make of Apollo (667-75)?

In what sense is Patroklos responsible for his own death (684-91; 705; 786-87)? What warning does Apollo give to Patroklos (707-9)? What aid does Apollo give to Hektor (715-25)? How is the simile in lines 752-53 an example of foreshadowing? How is Patroklos's death accomplished (791-821)? Why does Homer have Patroklos killed in this manner? What is the significance of Achilleus's helmet, which is struck off Patroklos's head and is picked up and worn by Hektor (796-800)? What prediction does the dying Patroklos make to Hektor (844-54)? What is Hektor's reaction to this prophecy (859-61)?

Book 18: Exercise

How does Achilleus react to the news of Patroklos's death (22-34)? What figure of speech is employed in line 22? What ironical fact does Thetis point out to Achilleus (72-77)? Explain the irony of her statement. What is Achilleus determined to do as a result of Patroklos's death (90-93)? What does this action entail for Achilleus (95-96)? How does Achilleus view his anger, which had led him to withdraw from the war (98-126)? What must Thetis do before Achilleus can return to battle (130-37)?

What message does Hera send to Achilleus (197-201)? How does Achilleus drive back the Trojans (203-31)? What does Achilleus's rout of the Trojans enable the Achaians to do (231-38)? What help does Hera provide (239-42)?

Summarize briefly Poulydamas's speech to the Trojans (254-83). What is Hektor's reaction to this advice (285-309)? Is Hektor correct when he says that Zeus's intention in allowing him to drive the Achaians back to their ships was to give him glory (293-95; see 1. 407-10)? Explain your answer. What comment does Homer make on the Trojan reaction to the speeches of Poulydamas and Hektor (312-13)? What promise does Achilleus make to the body of Patroklos (333-42)?

Explain Zeus's sarcasm to Hera in lines 357-59. How does Hera reply (361-67)? What obligation does Hephaistos owe to Thetis (394-409)? What request does Thetis make of Hephaistos (457-61)? How does Hephaistos react to this request (463-67)? What connections with the story of the *Iliad* do the pictures engraved on the shield suggest to you?

Imagery

When a series of related images (word pictures) appears in a literary work, the reader should be alert to the possibility that the author is expressing something important about his story and/or characters through the pattern of his imagery.[14] The *Iliad*, as a whole, and Book 22, in particular, give evidence of patterns of imagery that add significance to the narrative.

As Cedric Whitman in his book *Homer and the Heroic Tradition*[15] has shown, there is a network of fire imagery that extends throughout the *Iliad* and is connected with heroism, especially that of Achilleus. The fire imagery of Book 22 is a continuation of the image in Book 18, in which Achilleus appears at the ditch to frighten the Trojans with his war cry. This image is designed to strengthen the impression of Achilleus's destructive power. There, Athene causes a flame to issue forth from a cloud around Achilleus's head. The flame is, in turn, compared to a flare and signal fires originating from a besieged city (207-13). The image of the besieged city is a foreshadowing of what the city of Troy will soon experience after Achilleus kills its champion Hektor. Also, the armor that is made for Achilleus later, in Book 18, is created by Hephaistos, the god of fire, and on the shield are depicted images associated with fire: sun, moon, and stars. In Book 22 the fiery brightness of Achilleus's armor is compared to the destructive star Orion's Dog (Sirius), which rises in late summer when, as the ancients believed, oppressive heat caused disease

---

[14] *Imagery* is the employment of images (word pictures) in a given passage of a literary work, a whole work, or a group of works.

[15] (New York: W.W. Norton, 1965), pp. 128-47.

(26-31); and later Achilleus's spear is likened to the evening star Hesper, which seems to gleam especially brightly because of the darkening sky (317-18).

In Book 22 there are many other related images that contribute important significance to the narrative. Take careful note of this imagery and its meaning as you read this book.

Tragedy

The word *tragedy* is primarily used of a dramatic work, that is, a play in which a central character, called a tragic protagonist or hero, suffers some serious misfortune that is not accidental and therefore meaningless, but is significant in that the misfortune is logically connected with the hero's actions. Tragedy and its adjective *tragic*, however, can be applied to any literary work containing a protagonist whose actions lead to disaster for himself and others (as in the *Iliad*).

In tragic literature, the actions of the protagonist, no matter how well-intentioned, lead to disaster. In the *Iliad*, a sense of the futility of human action is conveyed by the use of dramatic irony, especially when Homer depicts his characters unknowingly doing things that lead them to their own doom and contrasts their ignorance with the gods' knowledge of their fate. In reading the *Iliad* note carefully how the actions of Achilleus and Hektor contribute to their own misfortunes and exactly when they become aware of the consequences of their actions.[16]

Book 22: Exercise

What does Apollo point out to Achilleus about his pursuit of the god (7-13)? What is Achilleus's reply (15-20)? What does the Orion's Dog simile emphasize about Achilleus (26-31)? Why does Priam urge Hektor not to fight Achilleus (38-76)? What is Hekabe's reason for making the same request (82-89)? What are Hektor's feelings about fighting Achilleus (99-110)? What does Hektor think about the possibility of making peace with Achilleus (111-30)?

What is Hektor's reaction to Achilleus's approach (136-37)? Note carefully the images applied to Achilleus and Hektor in the similes in lines 139-42, 189-92, 262-64, and 308-10. How are these images related, and what comment

---

[16] More will be said on the nature of tragedy in the introduction to Greek tragedy.

do they make upon these two heroes and the situation in which they find themselves? Explain what the images in the race and dream similes contribute to the narrative (159-64; 199-201). Why does Homer interrupt his account of the chase to describe the two springs (147-56)? What is the meaning of "Father" Zeus's balancing of the golden scales (209-13)? How does Athene help Achilleus (224-46; 276-77; 293-303)? What request does Hektor twice make of Achilleus (254-59; 338-43)? How does Achilleus answer him on both occasions (261-72; 345-54)? What does the dying Hektor predict to Achilleus (356-60)? What is Achilleus's reaction to this prediction (365-66)?

How do the Achaians and Achilleus treat Hektor's body (367-71; 396-404)? What comment does the simile in lines 410-11 make on Hektor's death? What does Priam decide he must do (418-22)? What did Hektor mean to Hekabe and the other Trojans (431-36)? Why does Homer describe Andromache's headdress when she faints at her discovery of Hektor's death (466-72)? What effect will Hektor's death have on his son, Astyanax (489-514)?

Book 24: Exercise

Describe Achilleus's psychological state in the beginning of the book (1-22). Why do Hera and Athene (the girl of the grey eyes) hate Priam and his people (25-30)? How is Achilleus's treatment of Hektor's corpse viewed by the gods in general (23-24)? by Apollo (33-54)? by Hera (56-63)? What role does Iris play in lines 77-88 and in lines 159-87 (as in 18. 166-67)? What request does Zeus make of Thetis (104-19)? How has Achilleus been living since Patroklos's death (128-31)? What is Achilleus's reaction to Zeus's message (139-40)?

What message does Zeus give to Iris to deliver to Priam (144-52)? What prediction does Zeus make about Achilleus's reaction to Priam's supplication (158)? In what condition does Iris find Priam (162-65)? What does Hekabe think of Priam's intention to go to Achilleus (201-16)? How does Priam answer Hekabe's objections (218-27)? How does Priam feel about his surviving sons (239-64)? What sign does Priam ask of Zeus (308-13)? How does Zeus answer his prayer (314-21)? What task does Zeus assign to Hermes (334-38)? Who does Hermes (Argeïphontes) pretend to be (390-400)? Where and in what condition is Hektor's body (411-23)?

What is the significance of the fact that Achilleus has resumed eating and drinking (475-76)? What does Priam do first when he enters Achilleus's dwelling (478-80)? What ritual act is Priam performing with these gestures? What is the irony of his kissing Achilleus's hands (478-80)? What arguments does Priam use to persuade Achilleus to return the body (486-506)? How does Achilleus react to Priam's acts and words (507-24)? According to Achilleus, what is the basic difference between divine and human life (525-26)? What is the moral of Achilleus's story of the two urns (527-33)? How does the experience of Peleus illustrate this moral (534-41)? What is Achilleus's reaction to Priam's impatience (560-70)?

In your opinion, why does Achilleus give Hektor's body back to Priam? Is it only because Zeus so ordered? Explain your answer. Why does Achilleus tell Priam the story of Niobe (601-20)? What connections can you find between the experiences of Niobe and Priam? How do Achilleus and Priam feel about each other (629-32)? What additional favor does Achilleus grant Priam (656-58)? Why does Hermes urge Priam to leave Achilleus's dwelling (683-88)?

What future does Andromache foresee for herself and her son (725-39)? What view of Hektor does Helen present (762-75)? Why does the poem end with the burial of Hektor? Do you find this an appropriate ending to the poem? Explain your answer.

Quadriga, an ancient chariot drawn
by four horses.
Acragas, c. 412–411 B.C.

Philosophical Background of the Fifth Century B.C.

From as early as the sixth century B.C., thinkers in Ionia[1] and elsewhere in the Greek world were speculating about what the universe was made of and how it came to assume its present form. These thinkers are conventionally called pre-Socratics.[2] This was the beginning of Greek philosophy, "the love of wisdom," which first took root in Ionian Miletus, a prosperous city on the coast of Asia Minor. The names of three Milesian philosophers are known to us: Thales, Anaximander, and Anaximenes, who are generally called the Milesians. We know of their teachings not first hand from their own works, which have not survived, but only from references to them in the works of Aristotle and other authors. Their main interest as philosophers is indicated by the term commonly applied to the Milesians and later pre-Socratics in Greek literature: hoi physikoi, "those concerned with nature" (physis). The physikoi sought the basic substance of the universe, but in addition to science, they were also interested in ethics and the criticism of contemporary religion. This kind of speculation was continued in Ionia, Italy, Sicily, and elsewhere by Heraclitus, Pythagoras, Empedocles, Democritus, and finally by Anaxagoras, who came to Athens in the middle of the fifth century. The greatest contribution of these philosophers was their application of rational analysis to the world, which had been previously viewed only in mythical terms.

The traveling teachers called Sophists, whose teachings had an enormous influence on the thought of the fifth century B.C., were, in general, intellectual descendants of the pre-Socratic philosophers. Perhaps because of the mutually contradictory answers offered by the pre-Socratics as to the nature of the universe, the Sophists turned from theoretical natural science to the rational examination of human affairs for the practical betterment of human life. This approach to life began to undermine the mythological view of the world evident in poetry, with its emphasis on the involvement of anthropomorphic deities in the natural world and in human action. Divine causation was no

[1] Ionia consists of the central portion of the western coast of Asia Minor, along with the islands off the coast. This area was inhabited by the Ionian Greeks, who had come from the Greek mainland to escape the Dorian invasions around 1,000 B.C. They spoke Ionic Greek, the basic dialect of the Homeric poems, which were composed in Ionia. Miletus, the home of the Milesian philosophers, was one of the principal cities of Ionia. See the map of Greece, preceding the chapter *Iliad*, for these and other important places.

[2] Socrates is commonly accepted as a turning point in Greek philosophy. As Cicero, the Roman orator, explains in his *Tusculan Disputations*: "Socrates was the first to summon philosophy down from the skies. . . and compelled her to engage in the investigation of. . . moral questions of good and evil" (5. 10).

longer the only explanation of natural phenomena and human action.

Most Sophists were non-Athenians, who attracted enthusiastic followings among the Athenian youth and received large fees for their services. Sophists flocked to Athens no doubt due to the favorable attitude of Pericles, the Athenian statesman, towards intellectuals. Pericles was a staunch rationalist; he had been trained in music and political affairs by Sophists. He was associated with the great Sophist Protagoras of Abdera and two important pre-Socratics: Zeno of Elea and Anaxagoras of Clazomenae. The latter taught that the universe was governed by pure intelligence, and his assertion that the sun, moon, and stars are red-hot stones and not gods led to his prosecution for impiety. Perhaps the best illustration of Pericles' rationalism is a story told by Plutarch of how Pericles, when an eclipse of the sun (generally considered a bad omen) frightened the helmsman of his ship, held up his cloak before the helmsman's eyes and asked him if he thought that this was a bad omen. Upon receiving a negative answer, Pericles then asked the helmsman whether there was any difference between his holding up of the cloak before his eyes and the eclipse of the sun except that the eclipse was brought about by an object larger than the cloak (the moon). Pericles was no doubt applying knowledge he had obtained from Anaxagoras, who is generally credited with being the first to explain the true cause of solar eclipses. Pericles' rational approach to life, and that of his circle of friends, was as unpopular as his democratic politics among conservative groups in Athens, but it must have encouraged Sophists from all over the Greek world to flock to Athens as a potentially fertile ground for their teachings.

Most Sophists claimed to teach *arete*, "excellence," in the management of one's own affairs and especially in the administration of the affairs of the city. Up to the fifth century B.C., it was the common belief that *arete* was inborn and that aristocratic birth alone qualified a person for politics; but Protagoras taught that *arete* is the result of training and is not innate. The Sophists claimed to be able to help their students better themselves through the acquisition of certain practical skills, especially rhetoric, the art of persuasion. Advancement in politics was almost entirely dependent upon rhetorical skills. The Athenian democracy with its assembly (*ekklesia*), in which any citizen could speak on domestic and foreign affairs, and the council of five hundred (*boule*), on which every Athenian citizen got a chance to serve, required an ability to speak persuasively. The Sophists filled this need for rhetorical training and by their teaching proved that education could make an individual a more effective citizen and improve his status in Athenian society.

Although there were many differences among the Sophists in terms of their specific teachings, it is safe to say that there was a common philosophy that many Sophists shared and that permeated their teachings. The most prominent element in this philosophy was skepticism, "a doubting state of mind." The skepticism of the Sophists took various forms: *phenomenalism*, the belief that we can know only ideas present in our mind, but not the objects of perception outside our mind (so that it is useless to make a definitive statement about anything outside our own mind); *empiricism*, the doctrine that experience, particularly of the senses, is our only source of knowledge; and, above all, *relativism*, the theory that truth has no independent absolute existence, but is dependent upon the individual and the particular situation in which one finds oneself.

The relativity of truth was the basis of Protagoras's rhetorical teaching. He trained his students to argue on both sides of a question because he believed that the whole truth could not be limited to only one side of a question. Therefore, he taught his students to praise and blame the same things and to strengthen the weaker argument so that it might appear the stronger. These techniques are based on the belief that truth is relative to the individual. Arguments on both sides of a question are equally true, because those debating a question can truly know only those things that exist in their own mind and, therefore, cannot make a definitely true statement about objective realities outside the mind (phenomenalism). Truth is what it appears to be to the individual. As Protagoras said: "Man is the measure of all things, of the things that are, that they are and of things that are not, that they are not." Since it is not possible to know what is absolutely true, there is only one standard left by which to determine correct action: the standard of advantage (interest, expediency). If an action is advantageous to the individual, then it is good. This idea was sometimes employed by the unscrupulous to justify morally questionable behavior, but Protagoras apparently was opposed to an indiscriminate use of this principle. His belief in the relativity of truth did not prevent him from believing that in making moral decisions one can still distinguish between an action that is morally better and one that is morally worse.

The Sophists were also interested in the cultural development of man as a member of society. The Sophists saw man himself as a product of nature, but society and civilization as artificial human products. On the one hand, man is a natural creature subject to certain laws of nature, which he cannot help but obey. On the other hand, he lives in a society, the rules and structure of which have no roots in nature and are based only on custom. The distinction apparent here is one between nature (*physis*) and custom or convention (*nomos*), a commonplace antithesis in fifth-century literature popularized by the Sophists. One of the great controversies of the fifth century was whether the gods, human society, and such distinctions among human beings as Greek and Barbarian, master and slave were the result of *physis* or *nomos*, nature or custom. Before the fifth century, human institutions and customs were generally seen as handed down by the gods and part of the natural order of things, but contact with other civilizations began to make it evident that institutions and customs were different among different peoples and introduced the idea of cultural relativism. According to this theory, societies create their own customs and institutions to suit their own peculiar needs and conditions. A graphic example of cultural relativism occurs in Herodotus's *Histories* (3. 38). In order to illustrate the point that everyone thinks his own customs and religion are the best, Herodotus tells the story of certain Greeks at the court of the Persian king who are shocked and disgusted when he asks them how much money they would require as an inducement to eat the dead bodies of their fathers. On another occasion, with Greeks present, the king asked some Indians, who in fact did eat their fathers' corpses, what they would take to burn their dead as the Greeks do. The Indians' horror at this suggestion equaled that of the Greeks on the earlier occasion. Herodotus concludes this anecdote with a quotation from the poet Pindar: "Custom is the king of all." This was also the attitude of most Sophists with regard to the origins of the gods, human society, and distinctions among human beings. All these were considered by the Sophists as human creations designed to serve specific needs. Thus there began to grow up the antithesis between man-made law (*nomos*) and natural law, which has its origins in unchanging nature (*physis*). A modern example of a *nomos* is the agreement that a red traffic light means stop while a green one means go; an instance of a natural law is the law of gravity. If a legislative body so ordained, red could mean go and green, stop. Under the right circumstances, the traffic light can be ignored with impunity. The law of gravity, on the other hand, cannot be repealed by man and compels obedience to itself.

    Although the *physis-nomos* antithesis was common in the teachings of most Sophists, their views of *physis* with regard to human nature could differ widely. To some Sophists, the realization that all men have much the same human nature required the abolishment of all artificial distinctions among men, for example, those between Greek and Barbarian or between master and slave. Other Sophists saw human nature as an aggregate of man's animalistic inclinations to aggression and domination by physical strength. Human law (*nomos*) that restricted those inclinations was seen as an artificial constraint contrary to the natural order of things, created by the weaker members of society. This view was the philosophical basis of the rhetorical argument of the right of the stronger ("might makes right"), which is used by a number of speakers in Thucydides' *History* and which you will see advanced by the Sophist Thrasymachus in Plato's *Republic*. The Sophists who advocated this argument saw men in the image of animals in the wild and often recommended the animal world as a model for the human. According to this view, any attempt to constrain the natural human tendency of aggression is not only wrong, but useless. Nature overrides any artificial constraints set up by man, just as, in the animal world, the strong will always be victorious over and dominate the weak. Not all Sophists, however, subscribed to this theory. Protagoras believed that men, left to their own natural savage instincts, would destroy each other. In his view *nomos*, although only an artificial creation of man, enables men to survive and makes possible civilized communal life.[3]

The intellectual revolution fomented by the Sophists also reached into the area of religion. Most Sophists saw the gods as creations of men. In general, Sophists were either agnostic or atheistic and saw the world as operating on the principle of natural rather than divine causation. There was very little room in Sophistic thought for the old anthropomorphic gods. This, of course, is not to say that the gods disappeared from ancient Greek life because of Sophistic skepticism. The Sophists and their students represented an intellectual minority. The average man, who could not care less about these avant-garde theories, distrusted intellectuals and regarded the agnosticism and atheism of the Sophists as irreligious and impious.

Protagoras was an agnostic, who claimed not to know whether or not the gods existed or anything about their appearance. Many other Sophists tended toward atheism. The Sophist Prodicus taught that men deify those things that are important to human life, such as the sun, moon, rivers, springs,

[3] In addition to the arguments of advantage and the right of the stronger, a third line of argumentation popularized by the Sophists was that of probability. This argument was especially useful in the courtroom, where the lack of evidence and/or witnesses made a charge difficult to refute. For example, a man charged with assault against a larger and stronger man could argue that it was not likely that he would have attacked such a person. On the other hand, if the man accused of assault were very large, he could argue that a man whose very size would make him a suspect would not be likely to have committed such a crime.

bread (Demeter), wine (Dionysus), fire (Hephaistos), and water (Poseidon), and at the same time (somewhat inconsistently from the modern point of view) the discoverers and providers of bread, wine, and fire (also called Demeter, Dionysus, and Hephaistos). Thus the goddess Demeter was considered simultaneously to be bread and the provider of bread just as Dionysus and Hephaistos were similarly viewed with regard to wine and fire. Another atheistic theory about the origin of the gods is attributed to a certain Critias, an associate of Plato, who was not himself a professional Sophist, but whose views were closely allied with those of the Sophists. Critias asserted that the gods were a contrivance of governments to insure that men would believe that everything done on earth, whether openly or secretly, was seen by the gods and would consequently be discouraged from violating the laws of the state. Otherwise, men, if not detected by other men, could break the laws of the state without fear of punishment. In this theory, belief in the gods brought stability to the state by providing sanction for its laws.

The ideas presented in this brief review of Sophistic teachings are commonplace in the late fifth-century and fourth-century literature. Authors in this course, for example, Thucydides, Sophocles, Euripides, Aristophanes, and Plato, give frequent evidence of the influence of the Sophists. The Sophistic movement represents an intellectual revolution that made educated men look at the world in a very different way. The Homeric view of the world and human events was no longer the only possible one.

Demeter, goddess of corn and of the
earth and its fertility.
Byzantium, c. 230–220 B.C.

Warrior
Lycia, c. 380–360 B.C.

The Peloponnesian War
Thucydides

Genre: History

What we refer to as myth or legend was considered historical fact by most Greeks down into and even beyond the fifth century B.C. For example, the Homeric poems were taken seriously as a historical record of the past. Indeed, as modern archaeology has shown, there is a kernel of historical truth in the *Iliad*; that is, a war did take place at the site of Troy in approximately the same period as was assigned to it by legend. Nevertheless, it is clear that the overall account of the Trojan war in the *Iliad* is the result of imaginative embellishment of a story told again and again by generations of poets. It was not until more than two centuries after the composition of the Homeric poems that a more scientific form of history developed.

Rational analysis, which had begun in Ionia with the Milesian philosophers with reference to the universe, gradually extended to include the recording of human events. *Historie*, the Greek word from which our word *history* is derived, means "inquiry" and indicates the nature of this new way of dealing with the past. The recording of human events was no longer the uncritical retelling of traditional myths and legends, but an account that was the result of critical evaluation applied to what the author himself and others had seen and heard.

As in the case of the *Iliad*, the medium for myth and legend was poetry. The artistic language of poetry adorned with various verbal ornaments suited well the re-creation of a legendary world that transcended ordinary experience. On the other hand, an account of the world, as everyone contemporary with the author saw and experienced it, needed prose, a less artificial language and the vehicle of everyday communication. Thucydides uses the term *logographers* to refer to the prose writers who came before and were contemporary with his great predecessor Herodotus (c.480-425 B.C.), and he criticizes them because they are:

> less interested in telling the truth than in catching the attention of their public, whose authorities cannot be checked and whose subject-matter, owing to the passage of time, is mostly lost in the unreliable streams of mythology (1. 21).[1]

Although their writings were flawed as history when judged by Thucydides' high standards, the logographers did not consider themselves story tellers in

---

[1] Quotations from Thucydides are translated by R. Warner (New York: Penguin Books, 1972). All other quotations are translated by the author. The number before the period refers to the book, and the number(s) after, to the section(s) of a particular book.

the epic tradition, but rather inquirers, whose aim was to convey the truth to their readers through the application of rational criticism to their evidence.

Only a few fragments of these prose writers survive, but there is one particular logographer, Hecataeus of Miletus, about whom we know more than any other. He was actively involved in Ionian politics during the time of the Ionian revolt against the Persians in the early fifth century and had traveled much in Asia and Egypt. His writings are typical of the logographers. He wrote a work called *Trip around the World*, which was a description of places and people he saw on a sea voyage along the coasts of the Mediterranean and the Black Sea. He also wrote a book called *Genealogies*, which dealt with the legends of various heroes and the families (including his own) that claimed descent from them. The most remarkable thing about his writings is the spirit of rational criticism that he applies to his subject matter. Hecataeus refused to accept gullibly the fantastic stories that had been handed down from time immemorial. His attitude is evident in the following fragment from his work: "I write what I consider to be the truth, since it seems to me that the Greeks tell many stories that are absurd."

Like Hecataeus, Herodotus, known as the father of history, was also a traveler. He was born in the Greek city of Halicarnassus in southwest Asia Minor, but left because of political troubles there. He lived for a while on the Ionian island of Samos, in Athens, and finally in Thurii, an Athenian colony in southern Italy. His travels outside the Greek world took him to southern Russia, Egypt, and the Middle East. In the manner of the logographers, his travels are reflected in his *Histories*, which contain accounts of various non-Greek places and peoples. Although Herodotus depended very heavily on the oral traditions of lands he visited, he also used literary sources. For example, he shows a knowledge of Homer and Hesiod and of the logographers, especially Hecataeus, of whom he is very critical.

Herodotus's history owes much to the spirit and organization of the Homeric epic. Like the Homeric poems, his work centers around various heroes, is characterized by a looseness of structure brought about by numerous digressions, and is organized around a central theme, the great conflict between the Greeks and the Persians in the early part of the fifth century B.C. Herodotus's purpose, however, is not only to preserve the memory of the great deeds of the past, but also to give a rational account of the cause of the wars. In the introduction to his work he refers to his history as "the publication of his inquiry" (*historie*). His purpose is not merely to chronicle[2]

---

[2] A *chronicler* is a writer who merely records events in chronological order.

events; he strives to find through inquiry a meaningful pattern in the events he narrates in order to make their significance clear.

On the other hand, despite Herodotus's more scientific approach to the writing of history, his view of the world is basically Homeric. Gods are still seen as involved in human actions. According to Herodotus, the Persians lost the war because of their king's attempt to exceed the limitations of his humanity, an act that aroused the jealousy of the gods and brought about his downfall. The distinction between myth and actual historical events is not yet as clear-cut in Herodotus as it is later in Thucydides. In the beginning of his work Herodotus cites the Persian account of the origins of the conflict between the Greeks and Persians involving the stealing of two Greek women, Io and Helen, by Asiatics and of two Asian women, Europa and Medea, by the Greeks in retribution. The rape of Helen led to the destruction of Troy, which aroused the hatred of all Asia (including the Persians) against the Greeks. All these events are quite clearly legendary, but Herodotus does not reject them on these grounds. Instead he refuses to express any judgment on their truth or falsity and then proceeds to assign the origin of the Persian wars to the injury that Croesus, a historical king of Lydia (in Asia Minor) in the sixth century B.C., did to the Greeks. Although Herodotus does not brand legend as mostly fiction, his work, as in the previous example, is, more often than not, based solidly on history. It remained for Thucydides to banish mythology totally from history and thus create the first scientific history.

Historical Background

In the sixth century B.C., the Greeks in Asia Minor had fallen under the control of the Lydian king Croesus, and later, when Croesus himself was defeated by the Persian King Cyrus, were forced to become part of the Persian Empire. In the years 499-494 B.C., the Ionians, led by the city of Miletus and aided by Athens and the Eretrians, attempted to revolt against Persia. After some initial successes, the revolt failed and Miletus was burned. Darius, the Persian king, did not exact severe retribution from the Ionians, but was determined to get revenge against the Athenians and the Eretrians. Herodotus reports that when Darius was informed of the Athenian involvement in the burning of a Persian city, he shot an arrow into the air, while saying, "Zeus, allow me to punish the Athenians," and ordering one of his servants to say three times every time he dined, "Master, remember the Athenians" (5. 105). In 490 B.C., Darius sent across the Aegean an invasion force, which was defeated by the Athenians on the plain of Marathon. In this glorious victory the Athenians lost only 192 men, while more than 6000 Persians died. Darius did not survive to launch another expedition, but his son, Xerxes, in 480 B.C. sent a massive force by land and sea with the object of conquering all of Greece.

The Greeks, under the leadership of Sparta, decided to make a stand against Xerxes' land forces at the narrow pass of Thermopylae in northern Greece. There 300 Spartans fought bravely, but were overwhelmed by the great numbers of the Persians, who were aided by a Greek traitor. The Athenians, realizing that the Persians were unstoppable on land, abandoned their city to the enemy, who burned the Acropolis. The Athenians, however, were able to fall back on their large fleet, which formed almost half of the Greek navy. Through the machinations of the wise Athenian leader Themistocles, the Greeks were forced to engage the Persians on the Bay of Salamis, off the coast of Attica, and in the ensuing battle defeated Xerxes' fleet. The victory was followed by the Greek defeat of the land army left behind by Xerxes at Plataea in 479 B.C.

The Greeks, led by the Spartan commander Pausanias, decided to pursue their advantage and liberate the eastern Greeks (chiefly the Ionians) from the domination of the Persians. After a significant Greek victory over the Persians in Asia Minor, the Ionians, who had been pressed into service in the Persian army, joined the Greeks. But the Greeks, soon finding Pausanias's dictatorial behavior intolerable, rebelled against their leader and asked Athens to lead them against the Persians. Athens gladly accepted the role of leader and undertook to form an alliance, under her own presidency, as an offensive and defensive pact against Persia. The Spartans welcomed the Athenian acceptance of this responsibility because they were not eager for a long-term involvement in eastern affairs and were, at that time, on good terms with the Athenians. The basic purpose of the alliance was to take revenge on the Persians for their invasions of Greece. The alliance has come to be known as the Delian League because the temple of Apollo on the island of Delos, a traditional center of Ionian worship, served as a meeting place for its assembly and as the location of the league's treasury. The Delian League included the islands of the central Aegean, the islands off the coast of Asia Minor, a few cities on the coast of Asia Minor, Rhodes, and some cities in Cyprus, Euboea, and the northern Aegean. At its height the league numbered two hundred member states. Most of these states were assigned a monetary contribution to the common fund of the alliance, while the more powerful states contributed manpower and ships. Although Athens would take the lead in case of war, in peacetime she was considered only a first among equals. She had only one vote in the assembly of allies, which determined policy of the league. In the ten year period 477-467 B.C., the alliance freed many Greek cities on the coasts of the northern Aegean and Asia Minor and expelled Persian garrisons.

While Athens was consolidating her leadership in the east, at home the walls around the city, which had been destroyed by the Persians, were rebuilt and the harbor of Piraeus was fortified. Sparta was alarmed by these fortifications, which were a clear sign that Athens with her strong navy and the resources of her allies was aiming to challenge Sparta for the leadership of the Greek world. Sparta's fears were soon justified. Athens openly revealed her imperialistic designs when she began to use the Delian League against other Greek states. In 472 B.C. she forced Carystos in Euboea to join the alliance on the grounds that this city was too near Athens to remain independent. Two revolts of member states followed in 469 and 465 B.C., which were dealt with effectively by the Athenians. Both cities suffered a fate that was to become typical of rebellious members of the Delian League: they lost their autonomy and were forced to pay tribute to Athens instead of making contributions to the alliance's treasury. Athens welcomed the opportunity to reduce free states to the status of subject states because, through governors or overseers and garrisons, they could exercise tighter control over these governments. Athens was also anxious to decrease the number of allies who contributed ships. It was more advantageous for her that free allies contribute money instead of ships because she could use that money to build ships, which nominally were the property of the whole alliance, but in effect became part of her own fleet. Many allied states, which originally contributed ships and manpower, gradually became less and less willing to endure the expense and rigors of military service. These states played into Athenian hands by voluntarily substituting money contributions for ships. Ultimately only three states contributed ships and for this reason remained, for most of the fifth century, important independent members of the league: Lesbos, Chios, and Samos.

After a disaster suffered by the Athenians at the hands of the Persians in Egypt, Athens dropped all pretense of equal alliance. The common treasury of the league was transferred from Delos to Athens in 454 B.C. The treasury, which had been under the allies' control, now became part of the Athenian treasury to be used in whatever way Athens saw fit. Other evidence of Athenian domination was the requirement that members of the league use only Athenian coinage and weights and measures, and that all significant court trials involving citizens of league member states be held in Athens. Perhaps the most offensive practice in the eyes of the member states was the settlement of Athenians, who retained their citizenship and allegiance to Athens, on purchased or confiscated land in allied states. These settlements enabled Athens, through surveillance by her citizens, to maintain tighter control in important parts of her empire. This practice not only served to keep subject allies in line, but was extremely popular in Athens because it provided land and financial opportunity for the poor.

In the early years of the Delian League, Athens was led by the democratic anti-Spartan Aristides, who was renowned for his fair assessment of allied monetary contributions to the alliance, and the pro-Spartan Cimon, who was one of the many aristocratic enemies of the democracy in Athens. After the death of Aristides in the early 460s B.C., Cimon was left as the most influential man in Athens, but the democratic movement there was too strong for him to maintain his influence. His power in Athens came to an end in the following way. While Cimon led an expedition to Sparta to help that city put down a revolt of her serfs, Pericles and a democratic colleague named Ephialtes introduced reforms that ended the political influence of a council made up of the two richest classes in the state. These reforms left the popular assembly, which was open to every male over the age of eighteen, in full control of the destiny of Athens and were welcomed by the middle and lower class Athenians as greatly diminishing aristocratic influence in government. Two other reforms of Pericles, pay for political offices and for service on juries, were enormously popular because they gave poorer citizens the opportunity for greater participation in the affairs of state. Cimon upon his return, in a general atmosphere of pro-democratic and anti-Spartan feeling, was ostracized.[3]

After the mysterious murder of Ephialtes in 461 B.C., Pericles, a strong advocate of imperialism, became the most influential leader at Athens. Under his leadership Athens extended her empire to include her immediate neighbors, Boeotia and Megara, the rich island of Aegina just south of Salamis, and the Achaian cities in the Peloponnesus. In 448 B.C., no doubt at the instigation of Pericles, Athens made peace with Persia. The purpose of this

---

[3] *Ostracism* was a political process whereby a politician whose policies had become unpopular could be banished from Athens for a period of ten years by a vote of the popular assembly. Ostracism was voted upon by scratching the name of a politician on a broken piece of pottery (*ostrakon*), which served as a ballot.

truce, in which Persia in effect acknowledged the sea empire of Athens, was to allow Athens to maintain her present control over her allies and subjects and to pursue any further imperialistic designs without the distraction of the Persian threat. With the conclusion of the Peace there was no longer any reason for the existence of the Delian League, but the Athenians were more determined than ever to hold on to their empire and to exploit the financial advantages it provided them.

Although it seemed that Athens had now very effectively consolidated her power, unrest threatened the stability of her empire. Boeotia, Megara, and Euboea soon revolted (447 B.C.). To add to the problems of Athens, Sparta took the occasion of the Euboean revolt to invade Attica, but inexplicably the Spartan forces withdrew without engaging the Athenians. Pericles, who had come back with his army from Euboea to deal with the Spartan threat, was thus able to return to Euboea and put down the revolt. The Athenians now realized that they must insure themselves against attack by the Spartans, as they had done with the Persians, and concluded a thirty-year peace treaty with the Spartans.

It was around this time that Pericles embarked upon a program of rebuilding the temples that had been burned in the Persian invasion. It was his policy that, since these temples had been destroyed in an invasion that was directed against all Greece, the building program should be financed from the treasury of the Delian League, which was now located in Athens. There was some resistance to this policy at Athens among politicians who not only disliked the democracy, but also were offended by the blatant imperialism of Pericles. This opposition, however, could not succeed in defeating an immensely popular building program that would beautify the city and provide employment for the masses. The assembly approved Pericles' plan and, as a result, the great classical monuments were built, which survive as symbols of Athenian imperialism: the Parthenon, with the colossal gold and ivory statue of Athene; the Erechtheum; the temple of Athene *Nike*, "Victory"; the impressive entrance to the Acropolis (Propylaea); the temple of Hephaistos; and the temple of Poseidon at Sounion.

During the last fourteen years of his life (443-429 B.C.) Pericles, with his political wisdom and eloquence, completely dominated Athenian politics. He was elected one of the panel of ten generals every year during this period, and although nominally his power was no greater than that of each of the other nine, the Athenians willingly committed their destiny to his direction. As Thucydides writes of the government of Athens at this time: "So in what

was nominally a democracy, power was really in the hands of the first citizen"
(2. 65). Pericles' policies were based on a simple idea: Athenian control over
her empire must be maintained at all costs. In pursuance of this aim, Pericles,
after a long siege, subdued the revolt of Samos (439 B.C.), an important independent ally and one of the few member states still contributing ships to
the alliance. Pericles dealt harshly with this threat to Athenian interests and
returned home a military hero.

Sparta and her Peloponnesian League decided not to intervene in the
conflict between Athens and Samos, but two incidents involving the Corinthian colonies of Corcyra and Potidaea brought Athens and the Peloponnesians
to the brink of war. In both cases Corinth (a member of the Peloponnesian
League) took offense at Athenian action. First, in 433 B.C., as a result of
a dispute between Corinth and Corcyra involving the latter's colony Epidamnus, Corcyra formed a defensive alliance with the Athenians, who then inter-
vened in a naval engagement between Corcyra and Corinth. Second, late
in 433 B.C., Potidaea, in the north Aegean and a member of the Delian
League, encouraged and militarily supported by her mother city Corinth, attempted to revolt from Athens. The rebellion was put down by Athens only
after a difficult two-year siege. Corinth, motivated by these offenses, in addition
to her traditional commercial rivalry with Athens, instigated the Spartans,
already distrustful of Athenian power, to initiate the hostilities that are the
subject of Thucydides' *Peloponnesian War*.

Exercise for Reading Comprehension and Interpretation

Introduction: Book 1. 1-23

Why did Thucydides choose to write a history of the war between Athens
and Sparta (1)? Why was life unsettled in primitive Greece (2)? Why did
Attica[4] achieve stability early (2)? What was the first collective action taken
by the Greeks (3)? What names does Homer use for the Greeks (3)? What
name was commonly used in later times (3)? What is the origin of this name
(3)? What was the achievement of Minos (4)? How did ancient Greek life
change from primitive to more modern times (6)? What effect did the acquisi-

---

[4] Attica is an area of about 1,000 square miles, of which Athens is the capital.

tion of wealth have on the Greek cities and relations among them (8; 13)? How was Agamemnon able to gather together the expedition against Troy (9)? Read carefully Thucydides' account of the logistical problems of the Greek army at Troy (11). Briefly compare in a very general way this account of the war with that of Homer in the *Iliad*. What is the most important difference in the way these two authors view the Trojan war? How did Corinth achieve prominence (13)? What was the most important result of the development of naval power(15)? What alliances developed in the Greek world after the Greek victory over Persia (18-19)?

What criticism does Thucydides make of Greek oral tradition (20)? of poets and logographers (21)? What is Thucydides' method with regard to the speeches included in his work (22)? with regard to his evidence (22)? What is his purpose in writing history (22)? What is his view of the cause of the war (23)?

Sparta

In the seventh century B.C., Spartan political and social life had undergone significant changes with the introduction of reforms (attributed to a legislator named Lycurgus) that made Sparta very different from other Greek states. Perhaps the most striking result of these reforms was that Spartan males from age seven were required to spend most of their life in a constant state of military training and preparedness. The Spartan devotion to military affairs produced a powerful infantry, which was renowned throughout the Greek world for its invincibility. On the other hand, Sparta's domestic situation prevented the development of a powerful navy because the relatively small number of Spartan citizens would have required the service of the much more numerous and potentially rebellious helots (serfs) as rowers on the ships, a situation that the Spartans would not tolerate.

The Spartan government created by the Lycurgan reforms was a combination of different principles of political administration. Unlike most other Greek states, the Spartans still had a hereditary kingship shared by two kings who were the supreme commanders of the army. In addition to the kings, the government was administered by a council of elders, an assembly, and five ephors (overseers), who were guardians of the people's rights. It is difficult to put one label on the Spartan constitution. The term *monarchy*, "government by a sole ruler," is suggested by the fact that Sparta had a kingship, but the sharing of the kingship is in contradiction of that term. The council, consisting of the two kings and twenty-eight elders over the age of sixty, which prepared business for the assembly and had great influence in all governmental affairs, gave the appearance of *oligarchy*, "government by a few." Since there was an assembly, in which every Spartan citizen (male) could vote, but not debate, Sparta might be called a democracy. But Spartan citizenship was restricted to a relatively small number, who controlled a much larger subject population, and the lack of debate was a serious curtailment of the assembly's powers. Thus Sparta was certainly not a democracy in the same sense as Athens.

The physical appearance of Sparta was quite deceptive. The Spartans lived in modest villages with none of the impressive monuments of a city like Athens. As Thucydides points out:

> Suppose, for example, that the city of Sparta were to become deserted and that only the temples and foundations of buildings remained. I think that future generations would, as time passed, find it very difficult to believe that the place had really been as powerful as it was represented to be. (1. 10)

The physical aspect of Sparta is a good example of the conservative resistance to change that had become one of her most prominent characteristics. Her conservatism was also evident in her extreme suspicion of strangers, which resulted in an ordinance forbidding foreigners to reside in Sparta for any length of time.

Sparta had been leader of the Greek world and champion of Greek freedom since the sixth century. Throughout that century she had driven out tyrannies on the Greek islands and mainland, including Athens. In the Peloponnesian War she again had the role of liberator with regard to the Greek states in the Delian League, which had fallen subject to the tyranny of Athens. Sparta, being a rather poor city, did not have impressive financial resources to support its efforts against the Athenians, who could rely on a seemingly bottomless treasury. But Sparta did have an important resource of her own: disciplined manpower and the aid of her allies in the Peloponnesian League, the oldest and ultimately the longest lasting alliance in the Greek world.

Exercise

The Debate at Sparta: Book 1. 66-78

Why does Sparta call a meeting of her allies (67)? What important criticisms do the Corinthians make of the Spartan character (68-71)? What picture do they paint of the Athenians (68-71)? What is the most important accusation the Corinthians make against the Athenians (68)? What is the main point of the Corinthian speech (71)?

What is the purpose of the Athenian reply (72)? What is the main point of the Athenian mention of Marathon and Salamis (73-74)? How did the Athenians acquire their empire (75)? What were their motives in so doing (75)? How do they defend their acquisition of empire (76)? How do the Athenians evaluate their own imperial rule (76-77)? What warning do the Athenians give to the Peloponnesians (78)?

Exercise

Pericles' Funeral Oration: Book 2. 34-46

Why is Pericles chosen to give this eulogy of the war dead (34)? What is Pericles' main purpose in this speech (36)? What does Pericles see as the political and social advantages of democracy (37)? What is the Athenian attitude toward law (37)? What pleasures in life are available to the Athenians (38)? What are the important differences between Athens and Sparta (39)? Summarize briefly Pericles' estimate of the Athenian character (40). What does Pericles mean when he says: "...our city is an education to Greece" (41)? What is Pericles' view of Athenian imperialism (41)? of women (46)?

Exercise

The Plague: Book 2. 47-55

What is Thucydides' purpose in recording the symptoms of the plague (48)? Compare this with his purpose in writing history (1. 22). What do the two purposes have in common? What effect did the plague have on the behavior of the Athenians (52-53)? Why did they behave in this way? What is the point of Thucydides' comment on the oracle about a Dorian[5] War (54)?

---

[5] The Dorians were a division of the Greek race, of which the Spartans formed an important part.

Exercise

The Policy of Pericles: Book 2. 56-65

What caused a change in spirit of the Athenians (59)? What is Pericles' view of the relationship between the interests of the state and of the individual (60)? According to his own estimation, what qualities of leadership does Pericles possess (60)? What does he see as the advantages and disadvantages of his policy (61)? as the real source of Athenian power (62)? How does he view the morality of the Athenian empire (63)? What is the result of the Athenian devotion to warfare (64)? What future profit is gained by enduring the present hatred of mankind (64)?

What are the important results of Pericles' speech (65)? Summarize briefly Thucydides' estimate of Pericles' leadership by listing his most important qualities as a political leader (65). According to Thucydides, how did leadership in Athens decline in the war years after Pericles' death (65)? According to Thucydides, why did Athens ultimately lose the war (65)?

Exercise

The Mytilenian Debate: Book 3. 36-50

What decision did the Athenians make about the punishment of Mytilene, on the island of Lesbos (36)? Why were the Athenians especially angry at Mytilene (36)? What was the Athenian feeling about the original decree the next day (36)? What do the Athenians decide to do as a result of this feeling (36)? How was Cleon originally involved in this affair (36)? How is he characterized by Thucydides (36)?

What criticism does Cleon make of democracy (37)? What are his views of law and citizenship (37)? How do his views of citizenship and political action contrast with those of Pericles (see 2. 40)? How does Cleon view the motivation and rhetorical techniques of his opposition (38)? According to Cleon, what purpose will the decreed punishment serve (39)? What view does he express with regard to the claims of pity and decency (40)? to the relationship between justice and Athenian interests (40)? In a good dictionary or reference work, look up the word demagogue. In what sense can Cleon be called a demagogue?

What is Diodotus's view of discussion before political action (42)? How does he deal with Cleon's insinuations of bribery with regard to his opposition (42-43)? What is Diodotus's primary concern (44)? How does he view the role of justice in this discussion (44)? the effectiveness of the death penalty (45)? of human nature and the sanctions of law (45)? According to Diodotus, what will be the result if Cleon's arguments convince the Athenians (46)? What is a better method of ensuring the security of the empire (46)? Compare this method with Pericles' method (see 2. 40). What does Diodotus see as the result if the original decree is carried out (47)? What is Diodotus's view of the claims of pity and decency (48)?

What was the decision of the Athenian assembly (49)? How did the Athenians prevent the punishment originally decreed from being carried out (49)? What punishments did the Athenians impose on Mytilene and on Lesbos (50)?

Exercise

Civil War in Corcyra: Book 3. 69-85

What two political parties were involved in the civil war? Which side was supported by Athens? by the Corinthians (69-81)? What pretext did the democrats use to kill the oligarchs (81)? What was their real motivation (81)? What atrocities were committed (81)? Of what political condition throughout the Greek world was the civil war in Corcyra the first example (82)? What comment does Thucydides make on morality in time of war (82)? What effect did revolution have on language (82)? Give one example of this phenomenon. What was the most important human motivation in time of revolution (82)? How was language used in civil strife (82)?

Give two specific examples of the general deterioration of character throughout the Greek world (83). What is Thucydides' view of man's true nature (84)? What happens to the general laws of humanity in civil strife (84)?

Exercise

The Melian Dialogue: Book 5. 84-116

What arguments do the Athenians say they will not use (89; compare 1. 73-74)? What is the Athenian view of the relevancy of justice to this affair (89)? To what standards of human behavior do the Melians appeal (90)? Why do the Athenians want the Melians to become part of their empire (95; 97)? What warning do the Athenians give the Melians about hope (103)? Why do the Melians have confidence in the support of the gods (104)? According to the Athenians, what universal law governs both the gods and men (105)? What is the Athenian view of the Spartans (105)? of Spartan justice and self-interest (107)? of honor (111)? What do the Melians resolve to do (112)? What was the fate of the Melians (116)?

Introduction to Greek Tragedy

Genre

As was noted in the discussion of the *Iliad*, the word *tragedy* refers primarily to tragic drama: a literary composition written to be performed by actors, in which a central character, called a tragic protagonist or hero, suffers some serious misfortune that is not accidental and therefore meaningless, but is significant in that the misfortune is logically connected with the hero's actions. Tragedy stresses the vulnerability of human beings, whose suffering is brought on by a combination of human and divine actions, but is generally undeserved with regard to its harshness. This genre, however, is not totally pessimistic in its outlook. Although many tragedies end in misery for the characters, there are also tragedies in which a satisfactory solution of the tragic situation is attained.

Reading Tragedy

Tragedy was a public genre from its earliest beginnings in Athens, that is, it was intended to be presented in a theater before an audience. Epic originally was also a public genre. Homer chanted the *Iliad* and *Odyssey* to the accompaniment of a stringed instrument called a *kithara* before an audience. Epic continued to be recited by rhapsodes at festivals like the Panathenaia, but it gradually became more of a private genre to be read from a manuscript at one's leisure. This happened in part also to tragedy. In the fourth century, Aristotle, in his *Poetics*, points out that it is possible to experience the effect of tragedy without public performance (that is, by private reading). Tragedy was still being written and produced in the Athenian theater in Aristotle's day, but the plays of the three great tragedians—Aeschylus, Sophocles, and Euripides—and no doubt of other playwrights were also being read privately. This, of course, is our primary means of access to ancient tragedy, except for occasional modern productions, which help us to a certain degree to appreciate its theatricality, but for the most part provide quite a different theatrical experience from that offered by the ancient productions.

Private reading of tragedy deprives us of the visual and aural effects, which were important elements of this genre. Our word *theater* is derived from the Greek word *theatron*, which contains the stem of the verb *theasthai*, "to view as spectators." *Drama* is a Greek word meaning "action," related to the verb *dran*, "to do." The author of a tragedy was not just a writer of a script. When his work was approved for presentation at the state religious festival called the City Dionysia (in honor of the god Dionysus), the state assigned him actors and a chorus. The author then had to perform the additional tasks of training the actors and chorus, of composing the music for the various songs of the actors and chorus, and of providing choreography for the chorus. Because we usually read tragedies rather than see theatrical productions of them, and because our reading is usually in translation, we miss the following elements that are additional aids to interpretation beyond the script of the play: scenery, inflection of actors' voices, actors' gestures and postures, costumes and masks, singing, dancing, and sounds of the original language with its various poetic rhythms. These handicaps, however, are no reason to neglect tragedy. We still have the most essential element of drama, the words, the playwright's most important medium of communication. According to Aristotle, "the plot is the soul of tragedy," and the plot is communicated to the audience primarily by means of words. You should, however, keep in mind that words are not all there is to tragedy. Use your imagination as much as possible in order to compensate for those elements lost in reading tragedy.

Tragic Festival

The Athenian theater was not a business enterprise like our theater, but was financed by the Athenian state as an integral part of an Athenian religious festival, the City Dionysia. Three tragic poets were chosen to present their plays by a magistrate called an *archon*, who had charge of the City Dionysia. Each one of the tragedians presented a tetralogy (a group of four plays), three tragedies and a satyr play,[1] on one morning of the festival. In the first half of the fifth century the three tragedies often formed a connected trilogy, which told a continuous story. One connected trilogy survives, the *Oresteia* of Aeschylus, consisting of three plays: *Agamemnon*, *Libation Bearers*, and *Eumenides*. This trilogy traces the story of the House of Atreus from Agamemnon's murder by his wife, after his return from Troy, to the acquittal of his son, Orestes, who killed his mother in revenge. Three other surviving plays of Aeschylus belong to trilogies, of which two plays have been lost. None of the extant tragedies of Sophocles and Euripides belong to connected trilogies, but are self-contained dramas. Although there is evidence that Sophocles wrote one connected trilogy, the normal practice of the second half of the fifth century was to write three unconnected tragedies.

The tragic poets competed with one another, and their efforts were ranked by a panel of judges. Aeschylus won thirteen first-place victories, Soph-

---

[1] The satyr play is so called because of its chorus, which consists of satyrs, grotesque woodland spirits having human form with a horse's ears and tail. Only one satyr play survives, the *Cyclops* of Euripides, which parodies the story of Odysseus and Polyphemus in the *Odyssey*.

ocles, twenty four, and Euripides, five. Euripides' relatively small number of victories is due more to his unpopularity among the Athenians because of certain radical themes in his plays than any lack of ability as a tragedian.

Athene, the virgin goddess of arts, crafts, and war, who favors Achilleus and the Achaians in the Trojan War (*Iliad*).
Thurium, c. 375 B.C.

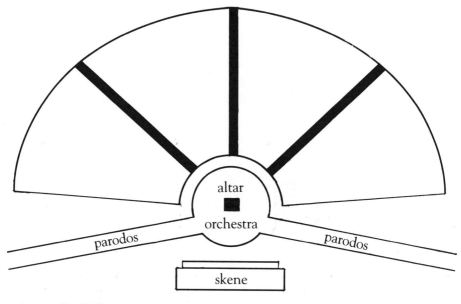

Ancient Greek Theater

Theater

The theater of Dionysus was, like all ancient Greek theaters, an open-air auditorium, and because of the lack of adequate artificial lighting, performances took place during the day. Scenes set at night had to be identified as such by the actors or the chorus; the audience, upon receiving these verbal cues, had to use its imagination. In general, the action of tragedy was well served by presentation in an open-air theater, since interior scenes, which are common in our typically indoor theaters, are all but non-existent in tragedy. The action of a tragedy normally takes place in front of palaces, temples, and other outdoor settings. This seemed natural to the ancient audience, because Greek public affairs, whether civic or religious, were conducted out of doors, as was much of Greek private life, due to the relatively mild climate of the Aegean area.

The theater of Dionysus in the earliest days of tragedy (late sixth, early fifth century) must have consisted of only the most basic elements. All that was required was a circular dancing area for the chorus (*orchestra*) at the base of a gently sloping hill, on which spectators could sit and watch the performance. On the other side of the orchestra, facing the spectators, there probably stood a tent in which the actors could change their costumes (each actor would play more than one part). This is suggested by the word *skene*, which means "tent" and which was used to refer to a wooden wall that had doors and was painted to represent a palace, temple, or whatever setting was required. The wall, which eventually became a full-fledged stage building, probably acquired this name because it replaced the original tent. The construction of the wooden *skene* (compare our theatrical terms *scene* and *scenery*) and of a formal seating area consisting of wooden benches on the slope, probably took place some time toward the middle of the fifth century. This was no doubt the form of the theater in which the later plays of Aeschylus and those of Sophocles and Euripides were presented. The actors positioned themselves either in the orchestra with the chorus or on the steps leading to the doors of the skene. The theater of Dionysus—as it survives today with the remains of an elaborate stone skene, paved orchestra, and marble seats—was built in the last third of the fourth century B.C. This stone theater had a capacity of approximately fifteen thousand spectators; the plays of Aeschylus, Sophocles, and Euripides in the earlier wooden theater were viewed by audiences of comparable numbers.

Two mechanical devices that were part of the ancient Greek theater deserve mention. One device is the *ekkyklema*, "a wheeled-out thing," a platform on wheels rolled out through one of the doors of the skene, on which a tableau was displayed representing the result of an action indoors (for example, a murder) and therefore was unseen by the audience. The other device is called a *mechane*, "theatrical machine," a crane to which a cable with a harness for an actor was attached. This device allowed an actor portraying a god or goddess to arrive on scene in the most realistic way possible, from the sky. The *mechane* deposited the actor on top of the skene so that he as a deity could address the human characters from an appropriately higher level. This device was not exclusively limited to use by divine characters, but was employed whenever the plot required any character to fly. On the other hand, not every god arrived on scene by means of this machine. The Latin phrase *deus ex machina*, "the god from the machine," is used in literary criticism to refer to a divinity who appears at the end of a tragedy to provide a solution for the plot and/or to prophesy what will happen to the characters. This phrase is also employed in a pejorative sense to refer to an improbable character or event introduced by an author to resolve a difficult situation. This secondary meaning of deus ex machina developed from the practice of inferior ancient dramatists, who introduced a god at the end of a play in order to untangle a badly snarled plot.

Actors

The actors in tragedy were hired and paid by the state and assigned to the tragic poets, probably by lot. In the extant plays there are never more than three speaking actors in the same scene. The three actors, in descending order of importance of the roles they assumed, were called the *protagonist,* "first actor," *deuteragonist,* "second actor," and *tritagonist,* "third actor." The protagonist[2] took the role of the most important character in the play, while the other two actors played the lesser roles. Since most plays have more than two or three characters, all three actors played multiple roles.

Since women were not allowed to take part in dramatic productions, male actors had to play female roles. The playing of multiple roles, both male and female, was made possible by the use of masks, which prevented the audience from identifying the face of any actor with one specific character in the play and helped eliminate the physical incongruity of men impersonating women. The masks with subtle variations also helped the audience identify the sex, age, and social rank of the characters. The fact that the chorus remained in the orchestra throughout the play, and sang and danced choral songs between the episodes, allowed the actors to exit after an episode in order to change mask and costume and assume a new role in the next episode without any illusion-destroying interruption in the play.

The main duty of an actor was, of course, to speak the dialogue assigned to his characters. This, however, was not the only responsibility of the actor. He occasionally had to sing songs solo or with the chorus or with other actors (for example, a song of lament called a *kommos*). The combination of acting and singing ability must have been as rare in the ancient world as it is today.

Chorus

For the modern reader the chorus is one of the more foreign elements of tragedy. The chorus is not one of the conventions of modern tragedy. We associate the chorus with such musical forms as opera, musical comedy, and oratorio. But tragedy was not just straight drama. It was interspersed with songs sung both by actors and chorus and also with dancing by the chorus. The modern parallel for tragedy is actually that form of opera (along with its descendant, musical comedy) where spoken words are interspersed with song and dance.

---

[2] In modern literary criticism, the term *protagonist* refers to the central *character* of the play, not to the actor.

The chorus, unlike the actors, were nonprofessionals who had a talent for singing and dancing and were trained by the poet in preparation for the performance. The standard number of members of a chorus was twelve throughout most of Aeschylus's career, but was raised to fifteen by Sophocles. The chorus, like the actors, wore costumes and masks.

The first function of a tragic chorus was to chant an entrance song, called a *parodos*, as it marched into the orchestra. The entrance song took its name from the two ramps (*parodoi*) on either side of the orchestra that the chorus used as it made its way into the orchestra. Once the chorus had taken its position, its duties were twofold. It engaged in dialogue with characters through its leader, the *coryphaeus*, who alone spoke the lines of dialogue assigned to the chorus. The tragic chorus's most important function was to sing and dance choral songs called *stasima* (singular=*stasimon*). The modern reader of Greek tragedy, whether in English or in the original Greek, finds it difficult to appreciate the effect of these choral songs that are now devoid of their music and dance.

Structure

Tragedy has a characteristic structure in which scenes of dialogue alternate with choral songs. This arrangement allows the chorus to comment in its song in a general way on what has been said and/or done in the preceding scene. Most tragedies begin with an opening scene of expository dialogue or monologue called a prologue.

After the prologue the chorus marches into the orchestra chanting the parodos. Then follows a scene of dialogue, called an *episode*, which in turn is followed by the first stasimon. The alternation of episode and stasimon continues until the last stasimon, after which there is a final scene of dialogue called an *exodos*, "exit scene." The exodos, in general, is a scene of dialogue, but, as in the case of episodes, sometimes songs are included, especially in the form of a kommos.

Here is the structure of a typical tragedy: prologue, parodos, first episode, first stasimon, second episode, second stasimon, third episode, third stasimon, fourth episode, fourth stasimon,[3] and exodos.

---

[3] Some tragedies have one more or less episode and stasimon.

Zeus, the ruler of the Olympian
gods, brother and husband of Hera
(*Iliad*).
Epirus, Pyrrhus, 297–272 B.C.

Antigone
Sophocles

Production

The setting of the *Antigone*, as in the case of most Greek tragedies, does not require a change of scene. Throughout the play the skene, with at least one door, represents the façade of the royal palace of Thebes. Even when the poet shifts the audience's attention from the palace to events in the plain and the cave in which Antigone was entombed, there is no shift of scene. These events are reported by minor characters (here, a guard and a character specifically called a messenger) rather than enacted before the audience (245-77; 1192-1243[1]). Interior action is also reported by a messenger to characters onstage for the benefit of the audience. The suicide of Eurydice, which takes place inside the palace, is reported to Creon (and to the audience) by a second messenger (1279-1318).[2] The messenger speech eliminates the need for scene changes, which, because of the limited resources of the ancient theater, would have been difficult and awkward to execute. Sophocles, however, like Aeschylus and Euripides, made a virtue of the necessity of this convention of the ancient theater by writing elaborate messenger speeches, which provide a vivid word picture of the offstage action.

Exercise for Reading Comprehension and Interpretation

Prologue (1-99): Antigone and Ismene

The play opens with the prologue, consisting of dialogue between Antigone and her sister Ismene. What is the dramatic purpose of the prologue? What problem does Antigone report to her sister (21 ff.)? What does Antigone intend to do? What is Ismene's reaction to this intention (49-68)? What is Ismene's view of the relationship between men and women (61-62)? Briefly analyze the characterization of these two women in the prologue. What dramatic purpose does the character of Ismene serve?

In the Greek text, the word *philos*, which can loosely be translated as "friend," is frequently used by the two sisters (10; 73; 99) in the prologue.

---

[1] The numbers are references to lines in the *Antigone*. All quotations from the *Antigone* are translated by the author.

[2] During the report of this messenger the body of Eurydice probably was displayed on the *ekkyklema* (1295).

Philos is related to the verb *philein*, "to love," and can be used as we use the word *friend*, but also can be applied to a blood relative, and therefore often means something like our "loved one." To whom does Antigone apply this term in the prologue (73)? How far is Antigone prepared to go on behalf of her loved one (72-73)? Why does Antigone, employing an oxymoron,[3] say that she will do "holy things criminally" when she refers to her proposed deed (74)? What conflict of values is represented in this phrase?

Parodos (100-161)

Although the events described in the parodos are presented rather obscurely in poetic language, as is characteristic of choral songs, can you summarize in a general way, in one or two sentences, what the Chorus is describing? The "man who had come from Argos" refers in a collective sense to the Argive army, which supported Polyneices in his attack on Thebes. Which side in the war does the Chorus favor and why?

First Episode (162-331): Creon, Chorus, and Guard

Creon, in his first appearance in the play, delivers a long speech outlining the philosophy that guides his actions and motivates his edict (162-210). What human institution does Creon believe to be most important in life? Compare his beliefs with those of Antigone. On what specific points does Creon contradict Antigone (182-83; 187-88; 209-10)? Note the language of Creon's edict (206-7). What character in a work read earlier this term used similar language with reference to a denial of burial?

What is the Chorus's initial attitude toward Creon's decree (211-14)? What is the dramatic purpose of the character of the Guard? How is he characterized in this scene? What view of Creon does the Guard present to us (228-36)? What is Creon's reaction to the Guard's news (280-314)?

First Stasimon (332-72)

The first stasimon, often referred to as the "Ode to Man," is one of the most famous choral songs in Greek tragedy. The Chorus begins by singing: "There are many wondrous things and yet nothing is more wondrous than man" (332). The Greek word for "wondrous" is *deinos*, which is ambiguous in its

---

[3] An *oxymoron* is a rhetorical figure of speech that joins two contradictory terms for paradoxical effect as in, "a wise fool." The word itself is a combination of two Greek words meaning "sharp-dull."

meaning. It can also mean "terrible" (that is, producing fear). The Chorus obviously intends the meaning "wondrous" when it praises man for his mastery of nature by the development of civilized skills. This praise of man's achievement of civilization is undoubtedly inspired by Sophistic anthropological accounts of man's cultural development as a result of his own efforts. Like the Sophists, the Chorus views human progress in an optimistic way.

Make a list of man's civilized skills as mentioned by the Chorus.[4] According to the Chorus, is there any limitation to man's mastery of nature (359)? Does it view man's cleverness as unambiguously wondrous, or is there also something terrible about it (368)? Explain your answer briefly. To whom is the Chorus referring in the last stanza of the ode when it sings: "whoever due to daring cherishes evil is without a city" (370-71)? Who appears onstage immediately after this ode? Connect the appearance of this character with what the Chorus sings in the last stanza of the "Ode to Man."

Second Episode (373-581): Guard, Antigone, Creon, Chorus, and Ismene

The second episode presents the face-to-face confrontation of the two antagonists, Antigone and Creon. What is the attitude of the Chorus and the Guard with regard to the capture of Antigone (373; 437-38)? How does Antigone defend her defiance of the edict (450-55)? How does Antigone view the relationship between laws made by man and those created by the gods? What is Creon's view of the relationship between man and woman and the relative importance of blood ties versus the ties of citizenship (484-85; 522; 525)? How does this contrast with Antigone's view of the same? What is Antigone's attitude with regard to her deed (502-3)? with regard to Ismene's attempt to share responsibility for the deed (538-60)?

Second Stasimon (582-625)

After the confrontation between Creon and Antigone, the Chorus sings of the misfortune that has come to Antigone and Ismene, who have been condemned to death. The Chorus puts this tragedy in the context of the calamities suffered by the House of Labdacus (592), the grandfather of Oedipus, who

---

[4] Note that Creon consistently uses metaphors (images) that link him with these skills and with civilization in general (189; 293; 476-78; 569). On the other hand, Antigone and the resistance to Creon's edict are generally represented by images associated with nature (423-25; 712-17; 825-30). Why do you think Sophocles organized his imagery in this way? What meaning does this organization of imagery suggest for the *Antigone*?

killed his father and married his mother, and whose sons, Polyneices and Eteocles, killed each other in a dynastic struggle. Who brought these disasters on the House of Labdacus (584-601)? Why has this family suffered so much and made such disastrous mistakes (613-25)?

Third Episode (626-780): Creon, Haemon, and Chorus

How would the Athenian audience have received Creon's statement to his son Haemon: "It is necessary to obey him whom the city puts in charge even in small matters, whether they are just or unjust" (666-67)?[5] How does the Chorus view this statement (681-82)? According to Haemon, what is the reaction of the common people to Creon's decree of death for Antigone (692-95)? What advice does Haemon give to Creon (707-11)? What is the point that Haemon is attempting to make to Creon by the analogies of the tree and the ship (712-17)? What criticisms does Haemon make of Creon (731-45)? What threat does Haemon make (751)? Why does Creon change Antigone's punishment from public stoning (36) to burial alive in a cave (773-80; see also 888-90)?

Third Stasimon (781-800)

What is the main theme of this brief ode to Love? Since choral odes generally comment upon the action of the previous episode, explain what connection this song has with the preceding scene. Can you find any lesson for Creon in this ode?

Fourth Episode (801-943): Antigone, Chorus, and Creon

What new side of Antigone's character do we see in the kommos that begins the fourth episode (808-82)? Antigone compares herself to Niobe (Tantalus's daughter), who because of her grief turned to stone (825-26). What does Antigone say that she and Niobe have in common (831)? What difference and similarity between the two does the Chorus see (832-36)? Antigone's statement in lines 905-12 has disturbed many critics of this play. For this reason, this passage has been seen by some as an interpolation made soon after Sophocles' death.[6] Other critics defend the authenticity of this passage by saying that

[5] Keep in mind that Solon, the Athenian lawgiver, had written: "You must obey the law of the land whether you think it right or wrong" (tr. Barnstone).

[6] This passage was in the text of the *Antigone* used by Aristotle in the fourth century.

these words are not as unfeeling as they seem: Antigone, on one hand, is talking about a real brother, who is now dead, and, on the other, a husband she has not yet married and children who do not yet exist. Which interpretation do you agree with? Why?

Fourth Stasimon (944-87)

The fourth stasimon presents three mythical examples that comment upon Antigone's situation. What do the first two mythic personages, Danae and Lycurgus (the son of Dryas), have in common with Antigone (944-63)? The third example, Cleopatra, may have also shared the same characteristic with Antigone, but it is not mentioned. According to C.M. Bowra,[7] these examples may indicate the doubts the Chorus has about Antigone. The Chorus has been alarmed by her defiant behavior, but it also has been impressed by her heroism. Bowra writes: "The three stories seem to suggest different interpretations of what is happening and to hint that any one of them may be right." Examine each example carefully and determine whether it puts Antigone in a favorable or unfavorable light.

Fifth Episode (988-1114): Teiresias, Creon, and Chorus

The fifth episode brings the appearance of the blind prophet Teiresias. What dramatic purpose does the character of Teiresias serve? What omens does Teiresias report (999-1011)? What do these omens mean (1023-33; 1065-90)? What is Creon's initial reaction to Teiresias's report (1034-47)? How is this reaction characteristic of Creon (see 294-303)? Why does Creon finally change his mind about Teiresias (1065-67; 1091-93)? What course of action does the Chorus recommend to Creon (1100-1)? What is Creon's reaction to this recommendation (1105-6; 1108-12)? What has Creon learned about law (1113-14)?

Hyporchema[8] *(1115-51)*

Why in the *hyporchema* does the Chorus choose to pray to Dionysus at this critical moment rather than to any other god? What request does it make of the god (1140-42)?

---

[7] *Sophoclean Tragedy* (Oxford: Oxford University Press, 1944), p. 105.

[8] An unusual feature of the structure of the *Antigone* is the substitution of a lively dance-song, called a *hyporchema*, for the more stately rhythms of a stasimon. The optimistic tone of the hyporchema has been occasioned by Creon's change of heart and is meant to emphasize by contrast the horror of Antigone's death and Creon's misfortune in the next scene.

Exodos (1155 to end): Messenger, Chorus, Eurydice, and Creon

Is the prayer of the Chorus in the *hyporchema* answered positively or negatively in the exodos? Why do you think Creon goes to bury Polyneices first rather than to Antigone's cave as he said he was going to do in the previous scene? What does Creon find when he arrives at the cave (1192-1225)? What is the result of Creon's confrontation with Haemon (1228-41)? In his kommos Creon gives voice to one of the traditional themes of tragedy. See if you can identify this theme in lines 1271-75. Why did Eurydice commit suicide (1301-5)? What moral lesson does the Chorus see in the fate of Creon at the close of the play (1347-53)?

Oedipus the King
Sophocles

Production

The setting of the *Oedipus the King*, as most Greek tragedies, does not require a change of scene. Throughout the play, the skene, with at least one door, represents in this case the façade of the royal palace of Thebes. Even when action takes place inside the palace, such as Jocasta's suicide and Oedipus's self-blinding, there is no shift of scene. These interior actions are described in a speech delivered by a messenger rather than enacted before the audience (1237-86[1]). The messenger speech eliminates the need for a scene change, which, due to the limited resources of the ancient theater, would have been difficult and awkward to execute. Action that takes place inside must also be reported by a messenger since indoor scenes cannot be realistically presented in the ancient theater. Sophocles, however, like Aeschylus and Euripides, made a virtue of the necessity of this convention of the ancient theater by writing elaborate messenger speeches that give a vivid impression of the off-stage action.

Exercise for Reading Comprehension and Interpretation

Prologue (1-150): Oedipus, Priest, and Creon

What is the dramatic purpose of the prologue? How does Oedipus characterize himself (8)? What is his attitude toward the suppliants (13-14))?

What conditions in Thebes does the Priest describe (25-30)? How do the suppliants view Oedipus (31-34; 40; 46)? The Priest refers to Oedipus's saving of Thebes from the Sphinx (35-38), a monster with a human female head and breasts and a lion's body with wings. The "tax" (36) that the Thebans paid the Sphinx was in the form of young men killed by the monster when they were unable to answer the riddle:[2] "What has one voice and four feet, two feet and three feet?" The answer, which only Oedipus was able to provide, was "man" (crawling on all fours as a baby, walking unaided on two feet throughout most of his life, and, finally walking with the aid of a

---

[1] The numbers refer to lines in the *Oedipus the King*.

[2] Although we associate riddles with children, these enigmatic questions were taken very seriously by primitive cultures and are often prominent in myths, which have their origin in a prehistoric era. Accordingly, riddle solvers were highly respected for their intelligence.

Sphinx of Thebes, who, according
to Greek legend, destroys all
passers-by who cannot answer her
riddle. Oedipus solves the riddle and
causes the Sphinx to kill herself.
Chios, c. 500–480 B.C.

cane in old age). What request does the Priest make of Oedipus (41-42; 51)? Dramatic irony is a much-used literary device in this play. Remember that the Athenian audience came into the theater already knowing the story of Oedipus and his horrible fate. Explain the irony of lines 60-61. What step has Oedipus already taken to deal with the problem (68-73)? According to Creon, what did Apollo[3] say must be done in order to cure Thebes of its pollution[4] (95-107)? According to Creon, what were the circumstances of Laius's death (114-23)? What motive does Oedipus assign to the killer of Laius (124-25)? What is Oedipus resolved to do (135-37)? Explain the irony of lines 137-41.

Parodos (151-215)

What is the reaction of the Chorus to the advice of Apollo (Delian Healer) to Thebes (154-57)? What conditions in Thebes does the Chorus describe (170-82)? The Chorus then asks Zeus to defend Thebes from Ares, who is usually the war god, but here is a god of destruction in general (190-202), and finally calls upon Apollo (Lycean King), Artemis, and Bacchus (Dionysus), who was born in Thebes, for help (204-15).

First Episode (216-462): Oedipus, Chorus, and Teiresias

Explain the following ironies in Oedipus's speech: lines 218-20, 236-48, 249-51, and 259-65. Why does Oedipus summon Teiresias (278-87)? What is Teiresias's reaction to Oedipus's request for help (316-44)? How does Oedipus view Teiresias's behavior (345-49)? What does Teiresias reveal to Oedipus as a result of the king's angry accusation (353; 362)? Note the emphasis on sight and blindness in the dialogue between Oedipus and Teiresias (see, for example, lines 367 and 371). What irony is implicit in this emphasis?

What suspicion does Oedipus begin to harbor about Creon (385-89)? What superiority does Oedipus claim over Teiresias (390-98)? Note the frequent equation of physical sight with knowledge throughout this scene and

---

[3] Creon had gone to obtain this information from Apollo's oracle at Delphi (also referred to as Pytho; Apollo himself is sometimes called Phoebus and Loxias), where the god's prophecies and advice were given to applicants by his priestess, the Pythia.

[4] A *pollution* is a religious uncleanness, which is usually the result of murder or of other serious crimes (intentional or unintentional) and infects anyone and anything that comes into contact with it. Because of the presence of Oedipus, a man polluted by the two terrible crimes of patricide and incest, Thebes is subject to a plague and other disasters.

the rest of the play. What is the irony of this equation? Teiresias then tells
Oedipus the horrible truth about himself (413-25). What does Teiresias predict
will happen to Oedipus (417-23; 452-60)?

First Stasimon (463-512)

What is the Chorus's view of Teiresias's accusations against Oedipus (483-95;
504-11)?

Second Episode (513-862): Creon, Chorus, Oedipus, and Jocasta

What motivates Creon's entrance at the beginning of this episode (513-22)?
Why does Oedipus accuse Creon of conspiracy (555-56; 572-73)? How does
Creon defend himself against Oedipus's accusation (583-604)? What does
Oedipus threaten to do (618-30)?

What does Jocasta attempt to do (634-68)? Is she successful (669-97)?
Lines 649-97 are sung by Oedipus, Creon, and Jocasta in conjunction with
the Chorus. That the characters break into song at this point is an indication
of their heightened emotions.

How does Jocasta try to assure Oedipus that he is not guilty of Laius's
death (707-22)? What is Jocasta's view of prophecy (723-25)? Why is Oedipus
frightened by the information given by Jocasta (726-45)? What happened to
the one surviving witness to the killing of Laius (758-64)?

Whom does Oedipus believe are his parents, and where does he think
he was born (774-75)? Why did Oedipus go to the Delphic Oracle, and what
was he told there (779-93)? Where did Oedipus arrive as a result of this information (798-99)? What happened at this place (801-13)? What does Oedipus
fear (813-22)? Does Oedipus suspect at this point that Laius is his father and
Jocasta, his mother (822-27)? Explain your answer. What detail in Jocasta's
story of Laius's death does Oedipus take comfort in (842-47)? How does Jocasta
try to reassure Oedipus (848-58)? What request does Oedipus make (859-60)?

Second Stasimon (863-910)

What wish does the Chorus express in the first stanza (863-72)? In the beginning of the second stanza the Chorus's statement that *hybris,* "arrogant pride,"
produces the tyrant is, without a doubt, a reference to Oedipus, since in Greek
the title of the play is *Oedipus Tyrannos.*[5] The Greek word *tyrannos* is most

---

[5] In addition, the word *foot* in line 878 is probably a reference to an etymology of the name
Oedipus presented later in the play—"swollen foot," a condition caused by the piercing of
his feet as an infant (1032-34).

often used in tragedy as a synonym for *king* and therefore usually has no pejorative meaning, but its use in this stasimon in connection with *hybris* suggests its other more sinister meaning in Greek, corresponding to what we mean by our word *tyrant*. In your opinion is Oedipus a tyrannical ruler? Is he guilty of *hybris*? If your answer to these two questions is yes, is he therefore responsible for his own fate? Explain your answer. In what way specifically can the words of the Chorus in the second and third stanzas (873-96) apply to Oedipus? What concern does the Chorus express in the fourth stanza ("the earth's navel" = the Delphic Oracle) (897-910)?[6]

Third Episode (911-1085): Jocasta, First Messenger, Oedipus, and Chorus

Jocasta appears alone on stage at the beginning of this scene. What prayer does she make and to whom is it directed (911-23)? After her prayer, the First Messenger arrives. What news does he deliver to Oedipus (924-63)? What is Oedipus's reaction to this news (964-72)? What is Jocasta's reaction (977-83)? What further information does the Messenger give to Oedipus (1008-46)? Whom does the Chorus identify as the herdsman mentioned by the Messenger (1051-53)? Why does Jocasta ask Oedipus not to seek out the herdsman and then leave (1056-75)? How does Oedipus interpret Jocasta's emotional behavior (1076-79)? What is Oedipus's view of the role of Chance (sometimes translated as Fortune) in his life (1080-85)? Is Oedipus's view correct? Explain your answer.

Explain the irony of the arrival of the Messenger occuring just after Jocasta's prayer. Is the Messenger's news really the good news he thinks it is?[7] Explain your answer.

Third Stasimon (1086-1109)

In the first stanza the Chorus addresses the mountain Cithaeron, on which Oedipus was exposed as a baby. In the second stanza the Chorus addresses Oedipus and speculates about the identity of his parents. Whom do they suggest as possible parents (1098-1101)?

---

[6] In connection with this stanza, it should be noted that the Delphic Oracle was not universally popular at Athens when this play was presented because Apollo was supporting the Spartans in the Peloponnesian War (Thucydides, 1. 118). Religiously conservative Athenians like Sophocles and Socrates, however, did not waver in their faith in the god.

[7] Be sure to read what Aristotle, in his *Poetics* (1452a. XI), has to say about the arrival of the First Messenger as the peripety of the play.

Fourth Episode (1110-85): Oedipus, Chorus, First Messenger, and Herdsman

By whom had the Herdsman been employed (1117-18)? Why is the Herdsman reluctant to answer the questions of Oedipus and the Messenger? What revelation does the Herdsman make (1128-81)?

Fourth Stasimon (1186-1222)

What general comment on human life does the Chorus make based on the example of Oedipus (1186-96)? Summarize briefly the account of Oedipus's life given by the Chorus in the next two stanzas (1197-1212). What horrible facts with regard to Oedipus's marriage does the Chorus point out (1214-15)?

Exodos (1223 to end): Second Messenger, Chorus, Oedipus, and Creon

What news does the Second Messenger announce (1235-79)? What is the symbolic significance of Oedipus's self-blinding (see, for example, the Teiresias scene and line 1484)? What does Oedipus intend to do (1290-91)? Why?

The next section of the exodos is a kommos in which Oedipus joins in song with the Chorus lamenting his fate (1297-1366). Whom does Oedipus blame for his sorrows (1329-31)?

What reasons does Oedipus give for his self-blinding (1369-85)? How does Oedipus feel about Creon at this point (1419-21)? What requests does Oedipus make of Creon (1436-37; 1446-67)? What future does Oedipus foresee for his two daughters (1489-1502)? What important truth about his life does Creon point out to Oedipus (1522-23)? What general lesson does the Chorus draw from the example of Oedipus's life (1524-30)?

Medea
Euripides

Production

The setting of the *Medea* does not require a change of scene. The skene, with at least one door, represents the façade of Jason's and Medea's house in Corinth. Even when the poet directs the audience's attention to events elsewhere, as in the case of the deaths of Creon and his daughter, in the royal palace, there is no shift of scene. These events are described in a speech delivered by a messenger (1136-1230[1]), rather than enacted before the audience. The messenger speech eliminates the need for scene changes, which, because of the limited resources of the ancient theater, would have been difficult and awkward to execute.[2] Euripides, however, like Aeschylus and Sophocles, made a virtue of the necessity by writing elaborate messenger speeches that provide a vivid word picture of the offstage action.

In the exodos of the play, Medea appears with the bodies of her children, in a chariot drawn by dragons, either on the roof of the skene or suspended from the *mechane*, in the manner of a deus ex machina.[3] She acts with the power, authority, and prophetic knowledge of a god from the machine when she establishes a festival and ritual in honor of her dead children, reveals her plans for the future, and prophesies the death of Jason (1378-88).

Exercise for Reading Comprehension and Interpretation

Prologue (1-130): Nurse, Tutor, and Medea

What is the dramatic purpose of the Nurse's speech (1-48)? The Nurse begins by referring to Jason's ship, Argo, which brought Medea to Greece from her home in Colchis (the Black Sea area). According to the Nurse, why did Medea sail with Jason (8)? What did Medea do upon arriving in Greece at Iolcus (9-10)? What is the present situation in Corinth (17-25)? What is Medea's attitude toward her children, and what does the Nurse fear she might do (36-43)? What rumor has the Tutor heard (70-71)? What is the Nurse's view

---

[1] The numbers refer to lines in the *Medea*.
[2] This explains why Creon rather surprisingly comes to Medea's house to deliver his decree of banishment (271 ff.) instead of summoning her to the royal palace.
[3] Since there are virtually no stage directions in the texts of tragedies, we cannot be sure which manner of presentation Euripides intended.

Pegasus, a winged horse, fabled to
have created the spring of
Hippocrene, a source of poetic
inspiration.
Siculo-Punic, c. 270–260 B.C.

of Jason's behavior (82-84)? the Tutor's view (85-88)? What feelings does Medea herself express (111-14)? What moral does the Nurse draw from the situation (119-30)?

Parodos (131-212): Chorus, Medea, and Nurse

The parodos is chanted by the Chorus, the Nurse, and Medea. How does the Chorus of Corinthian women feel toward Medea (176-83)?

First Episode (214-409): Medea, Chorus, and Creon

How does Medea view her situation in Corinth (214-24)? her situation as a married woman and mother (228-51)? as a foreigner (252-58)? What request does Medea make of the Chorus (259-66)?

What order does Creon give to Medea (272-76)? Why does he do this (282-91)? How does Medea reply to Creon's concerns (306-15)? How does Creon react to Medea's reply (316-23)? What request does Medea make of Creon (340-43)? What appeal does she make in support of her request (344-47)? What is Creon's reaction to her request (348-56)?

After Creon's departure, how does Medea explain her behavior (368-72)? What does Medea intend to do (373-85)? What problem is a concern to Medea, (386-90)? How determined is Medea to put her plan into action (390-94)? What is Medea's motivation (395-98; 404-5)? Medea's reference to her planning and contriving (402) would remind the audience of the meaning of the name Medea, "the cunning contriver." Her mention of her grandfather Helius, the sun god, calls attention to her divine ancestry (406). What is Medea's view of the female sex (408-9)?

First Stasimon (410-445)

What is the Chorus's reaction (410-20) to the last two lines (408-9) of Medea's speech? What comment does the Chorus make on the ancient poets' depiction of female faithlessness (421-30)? What is their view of Medea's situation (431-45)? To what is the Chorus referring when they mention the lack of respect for oaths and the absence of shame in Greece (439-40)?

Second Episode (446-626): Jason, Chorus, and Medea

What criticism does Jason make of Medea (446-58)? What does he intend to do for her and for his children (459-64)? What answer does Medea give to Jason's offer (465-72)? What had Medea done for Jason (476-87)?⁴ What accusation does Medea make against Jason (492-95; 510-11)? What is Medea's predicament (502-15)?

What is Jason's view of why Medea had helped him (527-33)? According to Jason, what advantages did Medea derive from coming to Greece with him (535-44)? What are the reasons that Jason gives for marrying the Corinthian princess (548-67)? What criticism does Jason make of women in general (569-75)? What criticism does Medea make of Jason's arguments (580-87)? What help does Jason offer Medea (610-14)? What is Medea's reaction to this offer (616-18)?

Second Stasimon (627-62)

What view of love (Cypris = Aphrodite) does the Chorus present in the first stanza (627-34)? What prayer does the Chorus make in reference to Cypris in the second stanza (635-41)? To whom is the Chorus referring in the third and fourth stanzas (643-62)?

Third Episode (663-823): Aegeus, Medea, and Chorus

What question did Aegeus ask of the Delphic Oracle (669)? What was the oracle's answer (679-81)? What request does Medea make of Aegeus (710-13)? What does Medea offer to do in return for Aegeus (715-18)? What is Aegeus's reply (723-24)? What is the only condition under which Aegeus will receive Medea into his land (Athens) (727-30)? What does Medea require Aegeus to do (731-32)? Why (734-40)? What is Aegeus's reaction to this requirement (741-45)? By whom does Medea make Aegeus swear (746-47)?

After Aegeus's departure why does Medea rejoice (764-71)? What will Medea do now with regard to Jason's intended bride (783-90)? What does she plan to do next (792-93)? What will she achieve through this action (794-806; 817)? What is her motivation in this action (797; 807-10)? Why, at this point in the play, has Medea decided on this form of revenge?

Third Stasimon (824-65)

What has occasioned this choral ode in praise of Athens ("descendants of Erechtheus" = Athenians)? What does the Chorus specifically praise in refer-

---

⁴ Pelias, fearful because of a prophecy that Jason would bring about his death, attempted to get rid of the hero by sending him on the quest for the Golden Fleece.

ence to Athens (824-45)? What does the Chorus ask Medea in the second half of the ode (846-65)?

Fourth Episode (866-975): Jason, Medea, and Chorus

What general attitude does Medea now present to Jason (869-905)? What is Jason's reaction to Medea's apparent change of mind (908-13)? How are lines 916-21 ironic? What does Medea want Jason to do (939-40)? How does Medea suggest Jason should go about this (942-43)? What will Medea do to help Jason in this endeavor (947-55)? What does Jason think of this help (959-63)?

Fourth Stasimon (976-1001)

What does the Chorus predict for Jason's intended bride, Jason, and Medea?

Fifth Episode (1002-1250): Tutor, Medea, Chorus, and Messenger

What news does the Tutor report to Medea (1002-4)? What is Medea's reaction to this news (1005-16)? Why does she react in this way? What reasons does Medea give why she should kill her children? Explain how Medea is ambivalent with regard to what she is considering (1021-80).

What is the Chorus's view of the parent-child relationship (1081-1115)? What specific relevance do these general comments have for the immediate situation of the play?

The Messenger reports the deaths of the princess and Creon himself to Medea. How were their deaths accomplished (1168-1221)? What general comments does the Messenger make on what has just happened (1224-30)? What does Medea intend to do now (1236-50)?

Fifth Stasimon (1251-92)

What prayer does the Chorus make to the Earth and the Sun (1251-60)? What warning does the Chorus give to Medea (1261-70)?

Exodos (1293-end): Jason, Chorus, and Medea

What concern does Jason express upon hearing of his children's deaths[5] (1326)?

[5] The murder of the children by Medea seems to have been an invention of Euripides. In other versions of the legend Medea does not murder her children. One version has Medea kill her children accidentally, while another has them killed by the Corinthians, and yet another has Creon's kinsmen kill them in revenge for Creon's death and circulate a rumor that Medea had murdered them.

What assumption does Jason make about the attitude of the Sun (Helius) toward Medea's action (1327)? Is he correct in this assumption? Explain your answer. According to Jason, why did Medea kill her children (1338)? What plans does Medea have for her children (1378-83)? for herself (1384-85)? What does she predict for Jason (1386-88)? What reason does Medea give for having killed her children (1398)? What comment does the Chorus make on the events of the play (1415-19)?

Grapes, associated with the god Dionysus.
Peparethos, c. 520–510 B.C.

Bacchae
Euripides

Production

The setting of the *Bacchae*, as with most Greek tragedies, does not require a change of scene. Throughout the play the skene, with at least one door, represents the façade of the royal palace of Thebes. Even when the poet shifts the audience's attention from the palace to events in the woods, there is no shift of scene. These events are described in three speeches delivered by messengers rather than enacted before the audience (434-50; 677-774 and 1043-1152[1]). Even when action takes place inside the palace, as in the case of Dionysus's humiliation of Pentheus (610-41), there is no shift of scene, but the god himself narrates this interior action to the Chorus. The messenger speech eliminates the need for scene changes, which, because of the limited resources of the ancient theater, would have been difficult and awkward to execute. In addition, these four speeches describe actions that could not be effectively portrayed onstage. Euripides, however, like Aeschylus and Sophocles, made a virtue of the necessity of this convention of the ancient theater by writing elaborate messenger speeches that provide a vivid word picture of the offstage action.

At the beginning of the third episode (576 ff.), Dionysus's words indicate the occurrence of various physical manifestations of his power: earthquake and partial collapse of the palace, lightning and a burst of flame from Semele's grave. It is difficult to say whether there was any attempt, or whether it was even possible, to present these events realistically. Perhaps offstage noises could have been used to represent the earthquake, but it is likely that the audience for the most part was expected to use its imagination.

Dionysus in his last appearance in the play (1330 ff.) is a deus ex machina, although, because of the lack of stage directions in the Greek text, we cannot be certain that he arrived by means of the *mechane*.

Dionysus and Dionysiac Ritual

The parodos is in essence a hymn sung by the Chorus[2] to Dionysus, which reveals various aspects of his divine personality and his ritual. Dionysus, especially under the Lydian name of Bacchus, became known as primarily a god

---

[1] The numbers refer to lines in the *Bacchae*.
[2] The Chorus consists of female worshipers of Dionysus, called *Bacchae*, whose name is derived from Bacchus, the Lydian name of the god. Female devotees of the god are often referred to as *maenads* (from the Greek verb *mainesthai*, "to be mad") and also as *bacchant[e]s*.

Dionysus, god of nature and the
theater, and the central character in
Euripides's *Bacchae*.
Mende, c. 425 B.C.

of wine in later tradition, but in the fifth century B.C. this was only one of his functions. He is a god of nature in all its vegetable and animal abundance. Dionysus is associated with ivy (106) and also with the oak and fir tree (110). One of his animal manifestations is that of a bull (619; 920), and *Bromius*, "roaring," a cult title used frequently in the *Bacchae*, may refer to his association with the bull and also the lion, although some connect this title with his lightning-struck mother.[3] Snakes, which were entwined in the hair of Dionysus's maenads (104), are another example of his connection with the animal world, as is his own and his maenads' attire made of fawnskin (136). The maenads' involvement with nature was also symbolized by a cane of fennel (a plant with a firm stalk), called a *thyrsus*, which they carried.

The primary rite of Dionysiac religion[4] was that of ecstatic mountain dancing. The culmination of this rite was a frenzy in which the dancers tore apart and devoured raw an animal, such as a goat or a fawn (136-37). These two acts are called respectively *sparagmos*, "tearing," and *omophagia*, "act of eating raw flesh." The rite of *omophagia* was seen as a communion with the god, in that the worshiper consumed a part of raw nature that was identified with Dionysus himself. The primitive rites of *sparagmos* and *omophagia* were still practiced in various areas in the fifth century B.C. and even down into Roman times, but in Athens, Dionysus was a much tamer god. There his worship was channeled into more civilized forms, such as the *Anthesteria*, a spring wine festival, and, of course, the City Dionysia. The Athenians seem to have concentrated on the pleasanter and more civilized aspects of Dionysus as a god of wine and of dramatic performances.

In the *Bacchae*, Dionysiac ritual is consistently connected with joy and freedom. The Chorus sings of the happiness of Dionysiac worship on the mountainside (64-82). The celebration of the freedom from all the constraints of civilization is summed up in the Chorus's wild Dionysiac cry "Evohe" and also represented in the simile at the end of the parodos, which compares

[3] In the *Bacchae*, there are references to the story of Semele's death by Zeus's lightning, his rescue of the baby Dionysus from his mother's womb, and the sewing of the baby into his own thigh in place of a womb to conceal Dionysus from Hera (88-99; 242-46).
[4] Dionysiac worship was one of the mystery cults that flourished alongside state religion in ancient Greece. The word *mystery* refers to the fact that these cults required that their rites be kept secret from outsiders (see 1108-9). The Greeks called the rites of mystery cults *orgia*, "orgies," but this word did not have the connotation of sexual license that the word carries today. There were some, however, like Pentheus, who suspected that the ecstatic Dionysiac rites led to sexual immorality.

the dancing of a maenad to the leaping of a colt (166-67).

One more aspect of Dionysus should be discussed here. He is a also a god of illusion. His powers of illusion are vividly demonstrated in the *Bacchae*. He deludes Pentheus on three different occasions: by making the king see him as a bull, think that the palace was in flames, and think that a phantom Dionysus, whom Pentheus was trying to stab, was the god himself (616-32). The god's ability to create illusions is one of Dionysus's traditional powers in myth and helps explain his connection with tragedy and comedy. Drama is based on illusion: dramatic action and characters are artificial creations of the dramatist presented in order to give the illusion of reality. Thus, it is appropriate that the god of illusion presided over the City Dionysia, Athens's dramatic festival.[5]

Exercise for Reading Comprehension and Interpretation

Prologue (1-63): Dionysus

The play begins with a prologue consisting of Dionysus's monologue addressed directly to the audience. What is the dramatic purpose of this prologue? Where was Dionysus born (2)? From what part of the world has he come to Thebes (13-14)? What is his purpose in coming back to Thebes (25-26)? What grudge does Dionysus hold against his aunts and the city of Thebes itself (27-31; 39-42)? How has Pentheus offended Dionysus (44-48)? What will Dionysus do after he leaves Thebes (48-50)? How will Dionysus appear in the play (54)? What is the main theme of the *Bacchae* as indicated by the prologue?

Parodos (64-167)

Next, the Chorus enters and the parodos begins. Who make up the Chorus of the *Bacchae*? What relationship does it have with Dionysus? From what geographical area does the Chorus come (64)? What is its attitude toward Dionysus (66-70)? What aspect of Dionysiac ritual does the Chorus emphasize throughout the parodos (76-77; 111; 132)?

---

[5] This discussion of Dionysus owes much to E.R. Dodds's edition of the play (Oxford: Oxford University Press, 1960).

First Episode (170-369): Teiresias, Cadmus, Pentheus, and Chorus

The first episode introduces us to Teiresias, Cadmus, and Pentheus. How are Teiresias and Cadmus dressed (176-77)? Why are they dressed this way? What reasons do these two give for accepting the worship of Dionysus (181-83; 200-204)? What is unusual about Teiresias and Cadmus behaving as they do (184-88)? What is Pentheus's general attitude toward the worship of Dionysus (215-48)? What does he suspect about Dionysiac rites (221-25)? What imagery does Pentheus use when he announces his intention to capture the worshipers of Dionysus in the mountains (227-32)? What relationship between man and nature does this imagery imply? What does Pentheus intend to do about the stranger from Lydia (239-48)?

What is Pentheus's reaction to Teiresias and Cadmus in Dionysiac dress (249-54)? What criticism does Teiresias make of Pentheus (266-71)? What explanation does Teiresias give of the nature of Demeter and Dionysus and of the myth about Dionysus being sewn into the thigh of Zeus (275-97)? In your opinion, does Teiresias's theorizing present an adequate representation of Dionysus? Explain your answer. What warning does Teiresias give to Pentheus (310-12)?

What reason does Cadmus give for accepting Dionysus as a god (333-36)? Do you find this a proper reason for accepting Dionysus as a god? Explain your answer. What does the fate of Actaeon (337-40) foreshadow with regard to the manner of Pentheus's death?

First Stasimon (370-433)

The first stasimon begins with an appeal to 'Holiness.'[6] What warning and recommendation does the Chorus make (387-401)? To whom do these words apply? Explain your answer. What is the Chorus's view of wisdom in this same stanza?

Second Episode (434-519): Attendant, Pentheus, and Dionysus

According to the Attendant how did Dionysus behave when captured (436-40)? What miracle does he describe (447-50)? What imagery does he use to describe the arrest of Dionysus (435-36)? What unmasculine characteristics does Pentheus find in Dionysus (455-57)? What attitude does Pentheus express with regard to the acceptance of Dionysiac worship among

---

[6] This is a poetic personification.

non-Greeks (483)? Explain the dramatic irony in lines 493-505. What flaw in Pentheus's character is especially evident throughout this scene?

Second Stasimon (520-75)

In the first stanza (520-36) of this stasimon the Chorus expresses its alarm at Pentheus's blasphemous rejection and arrest of the god. It asks Dirce, a famous Theban spring (here used symbolically for Thebes itself), why Dionysus and his worshipers have been rejected. Note that the Chorus uses the first person singular pronoun of itself as choruses often do, referring to themselves as a collective *I*. In the following stanza Pentheus is called a wild beast by the hostile Chorus (543). How is this another foreshadowing of Pentheus's fate?

Third Episode (576-861): Dionysus, Chorus, Pentheus, and First Messenger

What evidence of Dionysus' power is manifested at the beginning of this episode (576-603)? How does Dionysus humiliate Pentheus inside the palace (616-41)? What does Dionysus prove by this humiliation?

The description of the Theban maenads in the woods, presented in the First Messenger's speech (677-774), reveals two very different aspects of the Dionysiac experience. Explain briefly what these two aspects are. In your opinion why are the Theban maenads, once aroused, so violent and destructive in their behavior? Is this normal Dionysiac behavior? How does the view of the Dionysiac experience presented by the Chorus in the parodos and the first stasimon compare with the violent behavior of the Theban maenads? Does the Messenger's report support Pentheus's suspicions of promiscuity and drunkenness in Dionysiac rites (686-88)?

How does Dionysus tempt Pentheus to go to the woods (811-20)? What is the significance of Pentheus's dressing as a female worshiper of Dionysus (821-46)?

Third Stasimon (862-911)

The third *stasimon* begins with an almost Homeric extended simile of the fawn (866-76). What comment does this simile make on the relationship between man and nature? between Pentheus and Dionysus?

What is the Chorus's final definition of wisdom (877-81)? Has its definition of wisdom changed at all since the beginning of the play (386-401)? What does the image that depicts the gods as hunters of the unholy (890) foreshadow?

Fourth Episode (912-76): Dionysus and Pentheus

In the fourth episode what effect does Dionysiac possession have on Pentheus (918-22)? What does Dionysus's appearance to Pentheus as a bull tell us about his nature as a god? What is different about Pentheus's behavior in this scene as compared with earlier in the play? What is the irony in Dionysus's words in lines 963-66?

Fourth Stasimon (977-1023)

The fourth stasimon moves in its themes from the specific to the general. Try to identify the important themes of this ode. To whom does the Chorus refer in the first stanza (977-90)? What is the relationship between man and the gods depicted in this ode (1000-10)? What virtue does the Chorus stress (1004-10)? How does it define this virtue? What is the Chorus's view of Justice in the refrain (991-95 and 1011-15)? How do the themes of this ode connect with the action of the play?

Fifth Episode (1024-1152): Second Messenger and Chorus

What is the attitude of the Second Messenger toward the events on Mt. Cithaeron and the words of the coryphaeus (1024-40)? Compare the behavior of the Theban maenads, as described in the messenger speech (1043 ff.), with that related in the earlier messenger speech (677). What are the specific similarities? What imagery is both implicit and explicit in reference to Pentheus, his position in the tree, and the attack by Theban maenads (1095-1113)? What is ironical about this imagery?

What attitude does Pentheus express toward his behavior earlier in the play as he is about to be attacked by his mother (1118-21)? In keeping with the dominant imagery of the play, under what delusion does Agave labor at this point (1140-47) and in the following scene, in which she appears in person (1168 ff.)? What virtue does the Messenger stress at the end of his speech (1150-52)?

Fifth Stasimon (1153-64)

What is the main theme of this brief choral song? What emotional effect do you think that it was designed to produce on the audience?

Exodos (1165 to end): Agave, Chorus, Cadmus, and Dionysus

Explain the dramatic irony of the exodos. How does Cadmus bring Agave to her senses (1264 ff.)? Is Dionysus's revenge against Pentheus and Agave seen in the exodos as entirely justified? What is Agave's view in this regard (1301)? Cadmus's view (1249-50; 1302-08; 1346-48)? What punishments are imposed by Dionysus on Cadmus and his wife (1330-39)? In your opinion, why is Cadmus punished? What feelings does Euripides want to arouse in the audience by ending the play as he does? How do the closing lines of the play, chanted by the Chorus (1388-92), apply to the action of the *Bacchae*?

Poetics
Aristotle

Genre: Literary Criticism

Aristotle, who wrote on just about everything from metaphysics to botany, was the founder of literary criticism. His *Poetics* is the most important work of literary theory that has survived the ancient world and the most influential of all his works. It served as the basis of Renaissance poetic theory, and its influence has been felt even in twentieth-century literary criticism.

Aristotle wrote the *Poetics* about seventy-five years after the last of the great fifth-century tragedies had been written. His chief aim was to give advice on writing tragedy to contemporary poets.[1] Although Aristotle presents many examples from fifth-century tragedy to illustrate his theories, his view of the ideal tragedy is based on Sophocles' *Oedipus the King*. For this reason, Aristotle's theories are not always useful in the interpretation of other Greek tragedies.

Exercise for Reading Comprehension and Interpretation

VI. 2

How does Aristotle define tragedy? What emotions are aroused by tragedy? What psychological purpose does tragedy serve?

IX. 3-4

Why is poetry more philosophic than history? How does Aristotle define the universal? What is the aim of poetry?

IX. 11-12

What qualities should the incidents in a tragedy have?

X. 1-3

What are the two kinds of tragic plots? Explain how they are different from one another.

---

[1] Another of Aristotle's purposes in writing the *Poetics* was to answer the objections to dramatic poetry expressed by his teacher, Plato, in the *Republic*. Read sections 394c-398c and 602a-608b in that work, where Plato explains his reasons for banishing drama from his ideal state. As you read the *Poetics*, be careful to note how Aristotle responds to these objections.

XI. 1-5

What is a peripety?[2] What is a discovery?[3] What is the best form of discovery?

XIII. 2-3

What are the three forms of plot to be avoided? Explain why each is inappropriate to tragedy. What kind of plot best arouses pity and fear? Why does this kind of plot best arouse these emotions? In the ideal form of tragedy, what is the cause of the protagonist's misfortune?

---

[2] The Greek term *peripeteia* is sometimes translated as "reversal of fortune."
[3] "Discovery" is a translation of the Greek term *anagnorisis*, which is sometimes rendered as "recognition."

Introduction to Old Comedy

Genre

Three great comic poets in the fifth and early fourth century were recognized by ancient literary critics: Cratinus, Eupolis, and Aristophanes. No plays by the first two comedians have survived, but eleven of approximately forty comedies by Aristophanes are extant. The plays of Aristophanes represent the only surviving examples of a genre conventionally called Old Comedy.

The plots of Old Comedy have certain characteristics in common. They are not derived from traditional myth and legend, as is the case in tragedy, but are the concoctions of the comic poet. They are characterized by free comic fantasy. The most outrageous projects are presented as plausible solutions to contemporary problems. For example, in Aristophanes' *Lysistrata*, a group of Athenian women decide to persuade their husbands to make a truce with Sparta by refusing to have sex with them, and in the *Frogs* the god Dionysus, because of the lack of good tragic poets, decides to bring the recently deceased Euripides back from the underworld.

In Old Comedy, the contrast with the dignity and seriousness of tragedy could not be more marked. Slapstick action, scatological and sexual jokes, and just about every other device of humor known to man are found in Old Comedy. The purpose of this genre, however, goes beyond low farce. Political and social satire along with literary *parody*[1] are also characteristic of Old Comedy. For example, such political and intellectual figures from the contemporary Athenian scene as Pericles, Cleon, Socrates, and Euripides are targets of harsh comic censure. The Athenian people themselves are sometimes the objects of criticism. With regard to parody, the language of Old Comedy often mimics the high-blown style of tragedy for comic effect.

Hellenistic scholars in Alexandria first established the categorization of Athenian Comedy into three stages: Old, Middle, and New. One important basis of distinction among Old, Middle, and New Comedy is the prominence of the chorus. In Old Comedy the chorus plays an integral part in the drama. Middle Comedy, which first appears in the early fourth century, is characterized by a marked decline in the importance of the chorus and the absence of political satire.

In the late fourth century the development of the final stage of Athenian comedy, called New Comedy, is apparent. In New Comedy the absence of

---

[1] Parody is mimicry of the style of an author or genre for the purpose of ridicule.

the chorus (except for an occasional non-essential chorus) is notable. This form of comedy focused on family matters, such as complications in love relationships, with no interest in the concerns of the polis that were central to Old Comedy. Of the three stages of Athenian Comedy, New Comedy has had the greatest influence on modern comedy. The universality of human relationships that formed the subject matter of New Comedy allowed this form of comedy to translate well, first to Rome, then to Renaissance Italy and England, and eventually to our stages, movies, and television screens. Old Comedy, on the other hand, was tied to the political and social milieu of fifth-century Athens and therefore could not be as easily transplanted. But the spirit of Old Comedy still survives, for example, in modern political cartoons, occasional musical comedies, and comedy skits on television that satirize political figures and current trends.

The modern reader must be imaginative in trying to recreate in the mind a performance of Old Comedy, which, like tragedy, was very much a musical form, with singing and dancing by the chorus and actors. In addition, the understanding of the political and social context of a given play is essential to the appreciation of any Aristophanic comedy.

Comic Festivals

Old Comedy was produced along with tragedy at the City Dionysia, and also at a lesser Dionysiac festival in January called the *Lenaea*, "wine-vat festival." Before the Peloponnesian War, five comedies were produced at the City Dionysia, but during the war the number was limited to three.[2] In the latter period, on each of three days of the festival, a tragic tetralogy (three tragedies and a satyr play) was presented in the morning, and one comedy was put on in the afternoon. As in the case of tragedy, the archon chose the three poets whose comedies would be presented. A panel of judges ranked their efforts and awarded prizes. The comic poet also composed his own music and usually trained the chorus.

Theater

Old Comedy was presented in the same theater of Dionysus as was tragic drama, with the same background (skene), orchestra, and theatrical devices (*mechane* and *ekkyklema*).

---

[2] There was a similar reduction from five plays to three at the Lenaea.

Actors

Much of what was said in reference to the tragic actor in the matter of duties, the exclusion of women,[3] the wearing of masks, and acting style, also applies to the comic actor. There are, however, some important differences. Four speaking actors are often required in Aristophanes Comedy in contrast with the normal three in tragedy. The comic masks, which represented a variety of human and even animal figures, were comically grotesque. The masks worn by actors impersonating well-known Athenian figures, of course, bore a facial resemblance to those figures. The costume of the comic actor gave him more freedom of movement than that of the tragic actor. While the tragic actor was encumbered by heavy robes, the comic actor wore a short tunic, which allowed for the characteristically violent slapstick action of Old Comedy. Heavy padding of the costume produced a significant distortion of the human form. The grotesque appearance produced by this distortion, and also by the abnormally large leather phallus often worn by comic actors, suited perfectly the outrageous action of Old Comedy.

Chorus

The functions of the comic chorus remain essentially the same as those of the tragic chorus: to sing and dance choral odes and engage in dialogue with the actors in the person of the coryphaeus. The comic chorus had twenty-four members compared with the fifteen-member tragic chorus. Finally, the comic chorus often had to impersonate non-human characters, as is evident from the titles of Aristophanes' *Clouds, Wasps, Birds,* and *Frogs,* which were named after their choruses.

Structure

Although Old Comedy occasionally employs the tragic structure in which stasima act as dividers between episodes, it tends to favor the construction (found in early tragedy) wherein the stanzas of choral songs are separated one from another by interspersed dialogue, thus closely integrating choral song and dialogue.

---

[3] All speaking parts in Old Comedy were taken by men, but there were occasional silent parts for young women (for example, as slave-girls), which, because they required nudity, were played by females. The young women who played these roles were not respectable Athenian women, but slaves.

There are two elements that are regular structural features of Old Comedy: the *parabasis* and the *debate*. The parabasis, a long choral passage both recited and sung, during which the action of the play is suspended, is a direct address to the audience representing the views of the poet. Debate, in the general sense of a contest of words, is not peculiar to Old Comedy. Tragic dialogue often takes the form of a debate between two characters (for example, the contest of words between Dionysus and Pentheus in the *Bacchae*, 460-508), but the debate as a combination of speech and song is a readily identifiable feature of Old Comedy.

Old Comedy has a typical pattern of action. In the beginning of the play the main character conceives an outrageous solution to some problem. Opposition to his plan is overcome in the debate. The parabasis, since it has no organic role in the development of the plot, can come either before or after the debate. The plan then is put into action and the results are dramatized.

Clouds
Aristophanes

Production

The setting of the Clouds requires two doors in the skene, one representing Strepsiades' house and the other, the Thinkery, both in the city of Athens. The play begins with Strepsiades and Pheidippides sleeping in their beds. Since the ancient Greek theater had no curtain, these two men in their beds had to be carried out in full view of the audience by stagehands (probably slaves) and placed in front of one of the doors of the skene representing Strepsiades' house. The audience was no doubt expected to imagine that this was an indoor scene, because it was not usual for Greeks to sleep outside.

The method of presenting the scholarly activities that go on inside the Thinkery is by no means certain. K. J. Dover[1] suggests two possibilities. One is that the students could come out of the other door of the skene and carry with them their apparatus, which they could leave behind when they go back inside. Another possibility is that a screen made of canvas and wood, with a door held from behind by stagehands, could conceal the students until Strepsiades asks that the door be opened. The stagehands then could remove this screen, thus revealing the students and their equipment. When the students are ordered to go back inside, the door they go through would become the door of the Thinkery for the rest of the play.

One other aspect of production needs to be mentioned. In the play, Socrates first appears suspended in air. The means of his suspension is un-doubtedly the *mechane*, which in tragedy was mostly used for gods, but in comedy is used for any character who needs to fly or just be in the air.

Aristophanes' Comic Portrait of Socrates

Although there is something of the real Socrates[2] in the character of the same name in the Clouds, it is clear that Aristophanes' depiction of Socrates is a distortion. Socrates was a well-known figure in Athens who was popularly perceived as an intellectual. Aristophanes, taking advantage of this popular perception, arbitrarily places him at the head of the Thinkery, in which subjects such as rhetoric and astronomy are taught. As will become evident in the *Apology* and the *Republic*, Socrates was not a teacher of rhetoric or any of the other topics taught in the Thinkery. He was not concerned with

---

[1] *Aristophanic Comedy* (Berkeley and Los Angeles: University of California, 1972), p. 107-8.
[2] For example, the metaphor of midwifery (137 ff.); Socrates' shoelessness and endurance (363); his reduction of Strepsiades to a state of utter bewilderment (791 ff.).

teaching students to achieve material success through oratory; in fact, his main interest was to encourage young men toward spiritual, not material progress. Despite Socrates' atheism in the *Clouds*, he was not a scoffer at traditional religion, but a pious believer in the gods.

It indeed seems shocking that Aristophanes could so completely misrepresent Socrates, but in 423 B.C., when the *Clouds* was first presented, the distinction between Socrates and the Sophists might not have been as clear as it became later, when Plato, in the fourth century, began to write philosophical dialogues with Socrates as the central character. To the average observer at the time of the *Clouds*, Socrates did not seem terribly different from the Sophists. Like the Sophists, he was constantly seen in the company of wealthy young men, who, if they did not pay him regular fees, no doubt from time to time gave him financial support. Even if Socrates emphasized spiritual over material values, the actions of his young friends did not always reflect this emphasis, as in the case of Alcibiades and Critias.[3]

As Plato's depiction of him reveals, Socrates was not a typical Athenian. His rejection of such normal concerns of life as money made him seem quite abnormal. One reaction of society to the abnormal man is to laugh at him. Aristophanes, whether he knew the real character of Socrates or not, did not hesitate to take advantage of the comic potential of this unusual man.[4]

Exercise for Reading Comprehension and Interpretation

1. Scene (beginning with prologue): Strepsiades, Pheidippides, and Xanthias (slave) (1-132)[5]

The play begins with Strepsiades' monologue (prologue), which is interrupted by the sleep-talking of Pheidippides and two brief comments of a servant

[3] Alcibiades was a brilliant but unprincipled aristocrat, who, although an Athenian general, left Athens and helped the Spartans after he had been brought up on charges of impiety. Critias was one of the oligarchical Thirty whose reign of terror at Athens after the end of the Peloponnesian War brought about the death or exile of numerous democrats and the confiscation of their property.

[4] This discussion owes much to K.J. Dover's edition of the play (Oxford: Oxford University Press, 1968) and his book, *Aristophanic Comedy*, cited above.

[5] The numbers in parentheses refer to lines in the *Clouds*.

(1-79). What is the dramatic purpose of this monologue? What is Strepsiades' problem with his son (12-27)? with his wife (41-74)? What does his son's name mean, and why was he so named (63-67)? What salvation does Strepsiades see in the Thinkery (94-99)? Why does Pheidippides refuse to study there (102-4; 119-20)?

2. Scene (including parodos): Strepsiades, Student, Socrates, Students of Thinkery, and Chorus (133-510)

When Strepsiades arrives at the Thinkery, the Student speaks of the researches in the Thinkery as *mysteries* (143). He is referring to the secret knowledge and ritual that were known to only the initiates of mystery cults, like some Dionysiac cults and the Eleusinian mysteries.[6] Can you suggest a reason why Aristophanes uses the motif of mystery religion in reference to the education offered by the Thinkery?

What impression is given by the Student's description of the experiments in the Thinkery? What view are we given of Socrates before he arrives in person (144-74)? What is the physical condition of the students in the Thinkery, and what subjects do they study there (186-217)?

Socrates is suspended in the air in order to satirize the scientific theory (attributed to Diogenes of Apollonia) that connected thinking with air, both inside and outside the body. The air farther from the earth was considered purer and better suited for thought than that nearer the earth. What impression does Socrates give by his position and his words (223-34)?

Clouds are chosen as the chorus of this play and as patron divinities of the Thinkery because of the connection between clouds and various meteorological phenomena, such as rain, thunder, and lightning, in the scientific thought of some pre-Socratics. What are the different reactions of the Clouds when they see various men (348-55)? In reference to these reactions, in what sense can the Clouds be said to be moral critics? How is this view inconsistent with Socrates' first description of them (331-34)? What is Socrates' view of Zeus (367)? What has replaced Zeus[7] (379)?

---

[6] In Eleusis, a town in Attica about twelve miles from Athens, mysteries in honor of the agricultural goddesses, Demeter and Persephone, were celebrated.

[7] Socrates says that *Dinos*, "rotation," has replaced Zeus. *Dinos* has been variously translated as "Convection Principle," the "Whirl," "ethereal vortex," etc. This doctrine of the rotation of the universe was basic to the view of the universe espoused by the pre-Socratics Empedocles, Anaxagoras, and Democritus.

3. Parabasis: Chorus (518-626)

What view of the Aristophanes' style of comedy and that of his competitors is presented (537-62)? What complaint does the Chorus of Clouds make to the audience (575-94)? What offense have the Athenians given to the gods with the new calendar (607-26)?

4. Scene: Socrates, Strepsiades, Pheidippides, and Chorus (627-888)

Before Strepsiades, is allowed to study the immoral logic he is so eager for, he must study poetic meter and grammatical gender (636-93). Strepsiades finds great difficulty in understanding these subjects, and when he offends Socrates with the stupidity of his suggestion that he hang himself to get out of his debts, Socrates rejects him as a student (780-90). After this rejection, who suggests that Strepsiades send his son to the Thinkery in his place (794-96)? What does Strepsiades insist that his son learn there (882-85)?

5. Debate: Just Argument, Unjust Argument, Socrates, Strepsiades, Pheidippides, and Chorus (889-1114)

Next takes place the Debate between Just Argument and Unjust Argument,[8] which begins with unrestrained verbal abuse. What is the purpose of the Debate? Is the Debate absolutely necessary from a logical point of view? Explain your answer. What kind of education is praised by Just Argument (961-99)? What are the values that this education impacts to its students? Just Argument, while praising the modesty of the young men of his day, reveals an unusual interest in their genitals (973-78). Is this interest consistent with the general tone of his comments? Explain your answer. Compare the effects produced by the old education with those produced by a Sophistic education (1002-19)? What criticisms does Just Argument make of the effects of Unjust Argument's teaching (1020-23)?

What is Unjust Argument's basic approach to life (1036-42)? What aspect of human nature does Unjust Argument assume to be dominant in man when he, addressing Pheidippides, refers to "the necessities of nature" (1075-78)? What advantage will derive from being taught by Unjust Argument (1079-82)? Who wins the Debate? How is the winner of the Debate determined (1085-1102)?

---

[8] Translators render these names in various ways. However they are translated, the first speaker in the debate is usually given a name with a connotation of superior morality, and the second, inferior.

6. Second Parabasis: Chorus (1115-301)

What promise and threat does the Chorus make in the second parabasis?

7. Scene: Strepsiades, Socrates, and Peidippides (1131-1213)

What ability has Pheidippides acquired in the Thinkery? Give one example of the arguments that Pheidippides demonstrates to his father. Evaluate the logic of the argument.

8. Scene: Pasias (First Creditor), Witness, Strepsiades, and Amynias (Second Creditor) (1214-1302)

Strepsiades' creditors, Pasias and Annimas, arrive to get their money. Although Pheidippides was sent to the Thinkery to learn immoral logic for the purpose of cheating the creditors out of his father's debts, it is Strepsiades who unexpectedly routs the creditors. Perhaps this is an example of comic illogicality in a genre that does not require strict logic, or can you suggest a reason why Aristophanes makes this surprising substitution? What comic devices does Aristophanes employ in this scene?

9. Stasimon (1303-20)

What comment does the Chorus make on Strepsiades' success in getting rid of his creditors? Is this comment consistent with Strepsiades' and Socrates' perception of the role of the Chorus up to this point?

10. Scene: Strepsiades, Pheidippides, and Chorus (1321-1492)

Strepsiades gets his comeuppance when he is beaten by his son. In this scene Aristophanes is employing parody of tragedy. Strepsiades is shown here experiencing a sudden peripety in the manner of the tragic hero. At the height of his success (routing of the creditors) he suffers misfortune, as does Agamemnon in Aeschylus's tragedy *Agamemnon*, when, upon his return home after victory at Troy, he is murdered by his wife. Similarly, Oedipus suffers misfortune in Sophocles' *Oedipus the King*, when, as a respected and heroic king, he finds out that he has killed his father and married his mother. We are next presented with Strepsiades' realization of how he has been deceived by Socrates. When Strepsiades discovers[9] his guilt after being beaten by his

---

[9] Both discovery and peripety (reversal of fortune), mentioned in a few lines earlier, are terms of literary criticism derived from Aristotle's analysis of tragedy in his *Poetics*.

son (1476-77), Aristophanes is parodying a traditional theme of tragedy: learning by suffering.

What is the reason for Pheidippides' violence against his father (1353-76)? What is the implied contrast from Strepsiades' point of view between, on the one hand, the poetry of Simonides and Aeschylus and, on the other, that of Euripides? Given the patriarchal society of the Athenians, the beating of a father by his son was perhaps even more shocking to the original audience than it is to us. But Pheidippides then proposes to do something even more outrageous. What does he propose (1405), and what is specifically Sophistic about his proposal?

What is Pheidippides' view of law (1421-24)? What view of human nature is implicit in the example Pheidippides uses as a model for human behavior (1427-29)? What threat by Pheidippides finally makes Strepsiades realize the wrong he has done in sending his son to the Thinkery (1444-46)? Strepsiades then blames the Chorus for encouraging him in his immoral plans. What reply does the Chorus make to this accusation (1454-55)? What is the true role of the Chorus (1458-61)? What does Strepsiades' prayer to Hermes dramatically illustrate (1478-82)? What advice does Strepsiades report that Hermes has given him (1483-84)?

11. Exodos: Students of Thinkery, Strepsiades, Socrates, Chaerephon, and Chorus (Coryphaeus) (1493 to end)

What action by Strepsiades ends the play? What does this action illustrate with regard to Strepsiades? What effect did Aristophanes intend this action to have on the audience?

Lysistrata
Aristophanes

Production

The setting of the *Lysistrata* requires at least one door in the skene, representing the Propylaea, the monumental gateway to the Athenian Acropolis. All the action of the play takes place in front of this background.

An unusual aspect of the production of the *Lysistrata* is the use of two choruses, one of old men and the other of old women. The conflict between these two choruses forms an important part of the action of the play. In addition, there is a chorus of Spartans and a chorus of Athenians in the exodos.

Exercise for Reading Comprehension and Interpretation

1. Prologue: Lysistrata, Calonice (sometimes given as Cleonike), Myrrhine, and Lampito (1-253)[1]

What is the dramatic purpose of the Prologue? What problem is Lysistrata concerned with (33)?[2] What is Lysistrata's solution to this problem (124)? What will be the ultimate result if Lysistrata's solution is successful (148-54)? What does Lysistrata intend to have the women do (175-79)?

2. Parodos: Choruses of Old Men and Old Women (254-386)

What does the Chorus of Old Men intend to do (266-70)? What action does the Chorus of Old Women take against the men (331-86)?

3. Scene: Athenian Magistrate or Commissioner,[3] Chorus (Men), Lysistrata, and Three Women (387-466)

What is the Magistrate's view of women (387-420)? What does the Magistrate order the policemen to do (424-30)?

---

[1] The numbers in parentheses refer to lines in the *Lysistrata*.

[2] The *Lysistrata* is set in the same year in which it was performed (411 B.C.). The play reflects the disgust with war prevalent at Athens after she had suffered in 413 B.C. the loss of the whole fleet and most of the army that had been sent to Sicily. In addition, many of the members of the Athenian Empire had begun to revolt.

[3] The Magistrate (or as the title is sometimes translated, Commissioner) is one of a board of ten officials that temporarily replaced the Council of Five Hundred as chief administrative body of the Athenian government in the crisis after the disaster in Sicily

Aphrodite, goddess of love, who
favors Paris (*Iliad*).
Nagidus, c. 360 B.C.

4. Debate: Lysistrata, Magistrate, and both Choruses (467-613)

What reasons does Lysistrata give for the women having seized the Acropolis (488-92)? How do husbands generally react to women's criticism of the war (506-20)? What is the meaning of the wool-working analogy used by Lysistrata (567-86)? What concerns does Lysistrata have with regard to married and unmarried women because of the war (588-97)? What do Lysistrata and the other women do to the Magistrate (599-613)? What is the meaning of this action?

5. Stasimon: both Choruses (614-705)

In place of the expected parabasis, a choral song, in which the two choruses insult each other, is substituted. What fear does the Chorus of Old Men express with regard to the women's seizure of the Acropolis (626-35)? What complaint does the Chorus of Old Women make against the men (648-58)?

6. Scene: Lysistrata, Chorus (Women), and Three Women (706-80)

What has happened to hinder Lysistrata's plan (717-28)? What is the meaning of the oracle that Lysistrata reads to the women (770-76)?

7. Stasimon: both Choruses (781-828)

What is the significance of the examples of Melanion and Timon used by the Choruses of Old Men and Old Women (805-21)?

8. Scene: Lysistrata, Woman and Man (members of choruses), Myrrhine, Cinesias, both Choruses, and Spartan Herald (829-1013)

In what condition is Cinesias[4] as he arrives onstage (845 ff.)? What is the reason for this state? What does he want of Myrrhine (906 ff.)? What condition must Cinesias fulfill before she will comply with his desire (900-901)? In what condition is the Spartan Herald[5] as he arrives onstage (980 ff.)? What is the situation back in Sparta (998-1001)? What message for the Spartans does the Athenian Magistrate give to the Herald (1007-12)?

---

[4] The name of *Cinesias* and that of his municipality (*Paionidai*) are both derived from common street words for sexual intercourse.
[5] Like Lampito, the Spartan Herald speaks in the broad Doric dialect of the Spartans, which is often translated into English as an American southern dialect.

9. Stasimon: both Choruses (1014-42)

What view of women does the Chorus of Old Men express at first (1014-18)? What is the reaction of the Chorus of Old Women to this view (1019-21)? Explain how and why the Chorus of Old Men change their view of women (1022-42).

10. Exodos: combined Choruses, a Spartan, two Athenians[6], Lysistrata, Chorus of Athenians, and Chorus of Spartans (1043 to end)

What invitations do the combined Choruses extend to the members of the audience (1043-71)? In what condition are the Spartan Ambassadors as they arrive onstage (1076 ff.)? According to the Spartan, what is the purpose of the delegation (1080-81)? What advice does Lysistrata give to the Athenians and Spartans (1112-35)? According to Lysistrata, what had the Athenians done for the Spartans (1137-46)? the Spartans for the Athenians (1149-56)? What is the object of the sexual desire of the Athenian and the Spartan (1173-74)? According to Lysistrata, what will be the rewards of peace (1182-87)?

What does the first Athenian say about the relative merits of sobriety and drunkenness in political negotiations between the Athenians and Spartans (1228-40)? How does the play end?

---

[6] These two Athenians are sometimes identified as Cinesias and the Magistrate.

Apology
Plato

Genre: Oratory

Plato's *Apology*, is in the widest sense, an example of forensic oratory in which Socrates defends himself in court against his accusers. The *Apology* is also an important example of a fairly extensive literature designed to defend Socrates against his detractors and to present what his defenders believed to be the real Socrates. It should also be noted that the *Apology* is a set of three speeches re-created by a second party after the fact (like the speeches in Thucydides) and therefore should not be considered a word-for-word reproduction of what Socrates said on that occasion.

Historical Background

After the defeat of Athens by Sparta in the Peloponnesian War, the democracy, which had so vigorously prosecuted the war, could not survive. The Assembly, cowed by the presence of the Spartan fleet, voted to choose thirty men to form a temporary government while they created a constitution based on the ancestral laws.[1] The first step taken by the Thirty, with the tacit approval of the Athenian people, was to rid Athens of those politicians whose bad advice had contributed to Athens's downfall. But the ultimate aim of the Thirty was to eliminate their political opposition. Ignoring their assigned task of codification, they proceeded, with the support of the newly arrived Spartan garrison stationed on the Acropolis, to use their autocratic power against prominent democrats. Political ideology, however, was not the only motive behind the reign of terror established by these oligarchs, who became commonly known as the "Thirty Tyrants." Greed encouraged them to prey upon well-to-do Athenians by passing a law that they could put to death and confiscate the property of anyone not included on their list of three thousand citizens.

The tyrannical behavior of the Thirty resulted in a mass exodus of disenfranchised Athenians from Athens to neighboring cities. Among these exiles were the former generals under the democracy, Anytus and Thrasybulus. In the spring of 403 B.C. a small army of democrats led by these two men succeeded in entering the Piraeus (port of Athens) and, in the summer of the same year, defeated the forces of the Thirty. The remaining oligarchs were still in control of Athens, but the Spartan garrison, combined with the army of the Spartan king Pausanias, engaged in only token resistance to the

---

[1] The phrase *ancestral laws* was a well-known slogan of the oligarchs at Athens.

exiles. Through the efforts of Pausanias, the democrats were allowed to enter Athens peacefully, and the democracy was restored. An amnesty was decreed that stipulated that no citizen could be brought into court on a charge of political wrongdoing committed before the restoration of the democracy. The only persons excluded from this amnesty were the Thirty themselves and their close associates, who were outlawed. With the withdrawal of the Spartans, Athens again became an independent city.

Because the trial of Socrates took place in 399 B.C., four years after the restoration of the democracy, it must be viewed in the context of the events narrated above. Critias, the leader of the Thirty, and Charmides, who was his assistant, were known to have been, at one time or another, associates of Socrates. Socrates was tried under the auspices of the restored democracy, and although the actual prosecutor in his trial was the obscure Meletus, the prosecution was instigated by Anytus, one of the democratic leaders exiled during the rule of the Thirty.[2] Socrates had refused to become involved in the crimes of the Thirty (*Apology* 32c-d[3]), but the fact that he had remained in the city throughout the rule of the Thirty certainly did not endear him to the democrats who had gone into exile. This, of course, could not be the basis of an accusation in court because of the amnesty, but the charge could be couched in sufficiently vague terms to avoid a technical violation of the amnesty. On the other hand, Anytus and other enemies of Socrates almost certainly did not desire the philosopher's death, but would have been satisfied if Socrates had chosen the usual alternative of exile even before the trial had begun, or if he had proposed it as a penalty after condemnation. Socrates, however, refusing to be intimidated by the trial and insisting that his activities had benefited Athens, staunchly proclaimed his own innocence. His uncompromising attitude no doubt angered the jury and led to their decision to condemn Socrates to death.

Another factor to consider is the intellectual ferment at Athens during the last half of the fifth century. The fact that old beliefs were under constant

---

[2] It might seem strange that almost four years elapsed between the restoration of the democracy (403 B.C.) and Socrates' trial (399 B.C.). The reason is that a commission had undertaken the revision and codification of the laws, which originally had been the task of the Thirty, and until they finished their work in 400 B.C., the courts were in a state of confusion. Thus it is clear that the restored democracy sought revenge against Socrates as soon as it was practically possible.

[3] This number plus letter(s) refers to sections of the *Apology*. The numbers and letters are generally located in the margins of the text.

attack by intellectuals disturbed many Athenians. As early as the middle of the fifth century, Anaxagoras, who said that the sun and moon were not gods, was prosecuted for impiety, and rather than submit to the court's penalty (perhaps death), left Athens. In order to bring Anaxagoras to trial, a decree had been passed by the Assembly that virtually outlawed the teaching of astronomy as irreligious. This Athenian distrust of intellectuals, combined with the political pressures of the last two decades of the fifth century, made Socrates vulnerable to prosecution. Aristophanes, in the *Clouds*, had presented him as a Sophist and an irreligious teacher of astronomy, who corrupted his students with his teaching. Although Socrates was not a teacher of astronomy nor the impious man that he appears to be in the *Clouds*, he was a tireless questioner of traditional values and was seen constantly in the company of wealthy young men of oligarchic leanings. His enemies believed that Socrates was corrupting these young men with his radical ideas. In their minds, the actions of Alcibiades, Critias, and Charmides, which had been so disastrous for Athens in the last years of the war and immediately afterwards, confirmed that Socrates was a bad influence on young men.

The Historical Socrates

It is difficult to give an account of the real Socrates with total confidence because he wrote nothing and we are dependent on sources that are not at all impartial. For example, the *Clouds* of Aristophanes presents a hostile view prevalent among the Athenian populace during the last quarter of the fifth century. On the other hand, we have two apologies[4] for the life of Socrates, written sometime in the years immediately following his death, by two of his younger associates, Plato and Xenophon. These two works are the earliest examples of a tradition of literature in defense of Socrates, including a number of lost works extending down to the third century A.D., of which we know only the authors and titles. Plato's *Apology* presents to us three speeches, in the first person throughout, delivered by Socrates at his trial. Plato never intrudes to comment on what Socrates says. Despite the appearance of complete objectivity, it is certain that the *Apology* is not an exact word-for-word reproduction of what was said by Socrates on that occasion. On the

---

[4] The use of the word *apology* in this context is based on the meaning of the Greek word *apologia*, which does *not* mean "a statement of regret requesting pardon," but "a formal statement of justification or defense." The latter definition is in fact still a secondary meaning of our word *apology*.

other hand, since Plato was no doubt aware that his readers would include those who were present at the trial, the words he puts into the mouth of Socrates probably represent fairly accurately the essence of the original. Xenophon's *Apology* is a narrative in which alleged quotations from Socrates' speech are interspersed. There are no crucial differences in the views of Socrates presented by the two authors, who agree that Socrates was a noble character, unfairly judged by the Athenians.

There are, however, discrepancies. For example, the oracle from Apollo in Delphi, in Plato's *Apology*, says that no one was wiser than Socrates (21a). The same oracle in Xenophon stresses Socrates' moral rather than intellectual excellence. In the words of Xenophon's Socrates: "Apollo replied that no one is more free [that is, not enslaved by the desires of his body], more just, or more in control of himself than me."[5] Xenophon's Socrates, in his reaction to this oracle, confirms the truth of Apollo's statement, adding a claim of wisdom and, in general, revealing a conspicuous lack of the humility evident in Plato where he wonders about the meaning of the oracle (21b). The reason for this discrepancy may be the fact that Xenophon did not know Socrates as well as Plato and, more importantly, was not present at the trial while Plato was (*Apology* 38b). Although Plato and Xenophon certainly do not present impartial views of Socrates, it is generally accepted that a truer picture of the real Socrates can be found in the pages of their works than anywhere else.[6]

Socrates was not very physically attractive. He had a snub-nose, large protruding eyes that appeared to be continually staring, thick lips, and a pot-belly. Yet apparently he had enormous personal magnetism. As Plato has Alcibiades say in the *Symposium*: "Whenever I hear [Socrates]. . . my heart jumps and his words cause tears to pour down my face, and I see that very many others have the same experience" (215e).

Socrates was a man of his times in that he found handsome younger men sexually attractive. In Plato's *Charmides* he reports his own sexual arousal at the sight of the beautiful young Charmides (who later became involved with the Thirty Tyrants): "I caught a glimpse inside [Charmides'] garment and burned with passion" (155d). But Socrates took a view of love affairs between older

---

[5] All quotations in this section are translated by the author.

[6] In addition to the apologies of Plato and Xenophon, Socrates appears in almost all of Plato's *Dialogues*, in Xenophon's *Recollections* [of Socrates], and in two other works by these authors that both have the title *Symposium*, "Drinking Party."

and younger men that was atypical of the Athenian aristocracy: he believed that the purpose of this kind of love should not be sexual gratification, but the progress toward virtue of the younger partner. Socrates seems to have put this belief into practice throughout his life, even politely rejecting the sexual advances of the youthful and attractive Alcibiades, an unusual reversal of the normal relationship, in which the older man was expected to pursue the younger (Plato, *Symposium* 217a-219e).

Socrates' self-control went beyond the area of sex and was evident in his behavior as a soldier in the Peloponnesian War. Socrates made an enormous impression on Alcibiades with his ability to endure cold, his powers of concentration, and his coolness in crisis (Plato, *Symposium* 220a-221b).

Socrates' primary concern in life was arete, not in the Sophistic sense of practical efficiency in public life, but as moral excellence of soul, that is, virtue. Socrates, in fact, seems to have been the first philosopher to see the soul as the moral essence of the individual, improved by virtue and ruined by its opposite. Socrates' concern for morality involved not only the private sphere of a man's life, but also the public, as illustrated by his two involvements in politics. Both instances reveal him resisting injustice, on the one hand, of the democracy and, on the other, of the oligarchic Thirty. In 406 Socrates, serving as a member of the presiding committee of the Council, opposed the trying of the Arginusae generals as a group, instead of individually; and during the rule of the Thirty, he refused to become involved in their crimes by acting as their agent in the arrest of Leon of Salamis (*Apology* 32a-d).

One of the most famous doctrines associated with Socrates is that virtue is knowledge. Socrates thought that the kind of intellectuality that the Sophists were applying to the practical affairs of life should be applied to the moral life. One could not be virtuous, without first knowing what virtue is. Once one has attained the knowledge of virtue, then, according to Socrates, one cannot help but be virtuous, since no one does wrong voluntarily.[7] Socrates saw the elimination of ignorance as the first step in leading men to virtue. To this purpose Socrates evolved the technique for testing knowledge by argument and questioning that is known popularly as the Socratic method. The essence of this method is *elenchus*, a process that most often begins with Socrates' asking a question

---

[7] This was a very controversial point in philosophical circles from the last quarter of the fifth century down to the time of Aristotle. Socrates believed that men did evil only out of ignorance, while his opponents in this matter maintained that men often did wrong while knowing what was morally right.

of one of his interlocutors (for example, what is justice?). After a definition is given, Socrates gets the interlocutor to assent to a statement that obviously contradicts the first answer. The interlocutor then suggests another definition that is closer to the truth, but is shown by Socrates still to be faulty. This process may even be repeated a third time, until an acceptable definition is reached or it is felt that it is not profitable to go any further with the discussion. This is the technique that he used to point out the ignorance of his fellow Athenians and that his followers imitated, thus winning him many enemies (*Apology* 23a-e).

Despite his conviction that his fellow Athenians were ignorant, Socrates did not see himself as the possessor of the knowledge that others lacked. In his mind, his only wisdom lay in the fact that he realized that he didn't know anything worthwhile, whereas they, although ignorant, thought that they were wise (*Apology* 21d). Socrates' profession of ignorance is at least in part to be taken seriously in that he saw his philosophical function not as the presentation of a complete and coherent philosophical system, but as total involvement with his fellow man in the search for truth. This profession of ignorance, however, is also often an example of playful Socratic irony. The word *irony* is derived from the Greek word *eironeia*, "pretended ignorance."[8] Socrates frequently assumes this ironic pose in conversation with his younger associates in order to put them at their ease, since, given his skill at argument, philosophical discussion with Socrates could be an intimidating and inhibiting experience. Socrates, however, employs a more sarcastic kind of irony designed to confuse, when he is involved in discussion with more mature interlocutors (especially Sophists), who have an inflated sense of their own wisdom and self-importance. It was no doubt evident to many such opponents that Socrates was mocking them by continually answering one question with another. This practice produced angry reactions, as is evident in Thrasymachus's outrage at Socrates' irony in the *Republic* (336c-d).

At the heart of Socratic irony, however, was not just Socrates' playfulness, but a serious conviction that teaching was not, as in the manner of the Sophists, the mere handing over of information by the teacher to the student. In fact, Socrates did not consider himself a teacher in the usual sense, but only an assistant at the birth of knowledge, an intellectual midwife. In Plato's *Theaetetus*, Socrates uses this metaphor to explain how, although he knows nothing, he can help others in their search for truth: (150b-c):

---

[8] Our use of this word as a literary critical term (for example, *dramatic irony*) is entirely a modern usage.

I cannot give birth to wisdom myself, and the accusation that many make against me is accurate, that while I question others, I myself bring nothing wise to light due to my lack of wisdom. The reason for this is as follows: God forces me to serve as a midwife and prevents me from giving birth. (150b-c)

Unlike the Sophists, Socrates believed that knowledge was attainable, but in his view the only real knowledge is that which the student attains himself with the active use of his own mind. His purpose was to put young men on the right track toward truth and virtue; whether they attained these goals or not was up to them.

Exercise for Reading Comprehension and Interpretation

17-18a

What are the main themes of the introduction? What is the intended effect of this introduction?

18b-19

What are the older false accusations that Socrates mentions? What is the source of these accusations against Socrates? Why does Socrates find this older accusation harder to deal with than the one presently brought against himself?

20

When Socrates denies that he even attempts to teach others and that he makes money by such efforts, of what professional group is he refusing to be considered a member? What characteristic Socratic technique of argument is illustrated by his expressed admiration for the ability of Gorgias, Prodicus, Hippias, and Evenus to educate?

21-23

What was Chaerephon's question to the Delphic Oracle, and what did the priestess reply? What was Socrates' reaction to the reply? Since Socrates does not believe that he is wise, why does he not reject the oracle as false? What did Socrates proceed to do because of the oracle? What was his final interpretation of the meaning of the oracle? Explain why he adopted this interpretation. What does Socrates believe this oracle says about human wisdom? What duty does Socrates undertake as a result of the oracle?

24-27

What are the charges against Socrates brought by Meletus at this trial? Reread the three arguments that Socrates uses against these charges, and then explain how these arguments are typical of the Socratic method.

28-31

What meaning does Socrates' example from Homer's *Iliad* and his analogy of military service have for his present situation? What is Socrates' attitude toward the conflict between his responsibilities to his fellow Athenians and his divinely imposed duty? Explain the difference between the values emphasized by Socrates and those considered important by the typical Athenian. Look up the word *gadfly* in a dictionary. What is the meaning of Socrates' metaphor of the gadfly? According to Socrates, what is so unusual about his devotion to the highest welfare of Athens?

31-33

Explain the nature of Socrates' "divine guide."[9] How has this guide affected Socrates' life? What moral is illustrated by Socrates' service on the Council's executive committee and his conduct when ordered by the Thirty to arrest Leon of Salamis? In Socrates' view, what disqualifies him from being called a teacher, and why has he attracted such a large number of followers?

34-35

What usual practice of defendants in Athenian law courts does Socrates refuse to follow? Why does he find this practice objectionable? According to Socrates what would be impious about his earning acquittal by this means?

36-38b

When required to propose an alternative penalty, what does Socrates at first suggest? Why does Socrates reject exile as a possibile penalty? Why can't Socrates keep silent? Briefly explain the meaning of Socrates' statement: "an unexamined life is not worth living." What penalty does Socrates finally propose?

---

[9] This is F.J. Church's rendering of the Greek word *daimonion*, literally "a divine thing." See *Euthyphro, Apology, Crito* (Indianapolis: Bobbs-Merrill, 1980) p. 38. Other translators translate this term in various ways.

38c-42

What reason does Socrates give for his conviction? What prophecy does Socrates make with regard to the effect of his death on the Athenians? Why does Socrates assume that his condemnation is actually something good? What is Socrates' view of death? Why does Socrates especially want to talk to Palamedes and Ajax (son of Telamon) in the afterlife? Explain why Socrates, condemned to death, still believed that a good man can suffer no evil.

Two eagles on a hare. In Greek
myth the eagle, of the constellation
Aquila, is associated with
Ganymede, Aphrodite and Hermes,
and Zeus. The hare, commemorated
in the constellation Lepus, is said to
have been placed in the sky by
Hermes, in honor of its
fleetfootedness.
Acragas, c. 412–411 B.C.

Republic
Plato

Genre: Philosophical or Socratic Dialogue

After the death of Socrates, a number of his associates tried to re-create in a literary medium the philosophical conversations that he had engaged in with his followers. Their purpose was to give a more accurate picture of Socrates than that presented by his detractors and also, as in the case of Plato, to use these re-created conversations as a vehicle for philosophic investigation. Xenophon wrote a work called *Recollections* [of Socrates], which contains Socratic conversations interspersed with narrative by the author. In addition, Xenophon wrote a *Symposium*, "Dinner Party," which shares the same title and theme (love) with a Platonic dialogue, although the dramatic setting and the characters (except for Socrates) are different. A follower of Socrates, named Aeschines, also wrote Socratic dialogues, of which only fragments remain. Of course, the best known works in this genre are the twenty-three dialogues written by Plato; the *Republic* is an important example of this form.

Sophists, Athens, and Plato

The Sophists tried to teach their students how to live the most effective kind of life. They saw worldly success as the way to happiness. Socrates, however, was disturbed by the Sophists' emphasis on material values and by the amorality of their teachings. He believed that man must make morality his ultimate concern in order to achieve true happiness.

Plato, too, was troubled by Sophistic doctrines and by the way the average Athenian let himself be guided by values, whether Sophistic or traditional, that were not subjected to critical analysis. Plato believed that the Sophistic stress on the relativity of truth undermined morality. This scepticism about the possibility of knowing the truth led Sophists to teach that there was no infallible guide for human action beyond the principle of self-interest. It was clear to Plato that the average man, who could not explain to himself or to others why the rules of morality should be obeyed in a given situation, would certainly follow the dictates of his self-interest rather than any external moral standard. To Plato, this was a dangerous state of affairs, which leads to moral chaos. Plato believed that morality must be based on objective truth and must be reconciled with self-interest: that is, morality must be shown to be in the interest of the individual.

Plato also disagreed with the Sophistic view of human nature and society. According to some Sophists, the most basic law of nature was that the strong dominate the weak[1] and that this law of nature quite properly overrode any law of human creation (nomos) seeking to protect the weak against the strong. This doctrine is based on the idea that human society is just an extension of the animal world. In fact, irrational animal nature was used by some Sophists as a model for human behavior.[2] Irrationality is seen as a dominant element in human nature. An example of this view can be found in Thucydides' account of the Corcyraean revolution:

> Then, with the ordinary conventions of civilized life thrown into confusion, human nature . . . showed itself proudly in its true colours, as something incapable of controlling passion, insubordinate to the idea of justice. (3.84)[3]

Plato, however, saw man's true nature as rational and that civilized life must be conducted according to rational principles.

Although Sophistic doctrines aimed at producing happiness for man, Plato believed that they produced the exact opposite because of the erroneous view of human nature implicit in them. In Plato's view, the average man mistakenly identified his self-interest with the satisfaction of his irrational desires, whereas man's real self-interest and fulfillment of his true nature lay in the control of the irrational desires by reason. Therefore, Plato was determined to show that it is a violation of man's true nature to allow irrational desires to dominate reason. He believed that the supremacy of the irrational results in immorality and unhappiness. If this could be established, morality would be shown to have its sanction in human nature. It would be clear that wrongdoers automatically suffer because of their immorality and that morality brings its own reward. This line of reasoning would provide the most compelling argument for moral behavior.

But Plato's concern with morality led him beyond the individual to a consideration of political theory. Morality involves interaction with others, and therefore the organization of society and the nature of government are also central issues. He had lived under a democratic form of government at Athens and believed that it had failed Athens at a critical moment in the last years of the Peloponnesian War. Plato saw the Athenian democracy as an amateur government with citizens at the same time pursuing their own livelihoods and participating in political decision-making. The army was a

---

[1] See Thucydides' Melian Dialogue.
[2] See Pheidippides' use of the model of rooster society in the Clouds.
[3] All quotations from Thucydides are from R. Warner's translation (New York: Penguin, 1972).

citizen militia, which also required the individual citizen to serve a double role. In his mind, another danger in this system was that the economic self-interest of those in power often influenced their political decisions. According to Thucydides, self-interest had adversely affected the quality of leadership in Athens after the death of Pericles:

> . . . after [Pericles'] death his foresight with regard to the war became even more evident. For Pericles had said that Athens would be victorious if she bided her time and took care of her navy. . . . But his successors did the exact opposite, and in other matters, which apparently had no connection with war, private ambition and private profit led to policies that were bad both for the Athenians themselves and for their allies. (2.65)

Degeneration of leadership is brought about by the leader identifying the interest of his own office with his own profit and not with the welfare of the governed. For Plato, economic self-interest and political power must be kept separate and not be allowed to work in combination to the disadvantage of the state.

Plato believed that not only the democracy, but also the oligarchy of the Thirty, had gone astray, because political leaders, blinded by their own self-interests, neglected the interest of the state as a whole. Political power seemed to attract persons who lacked the prerequisite qualities of leadership: intelligence, integrity, and selfless concern for the welfare of the governed. Intelligence is central to the Platonic view of leadership. Qualification for the wielding of political power must be based on the possession of superior intelligence, not superior physical force. From intelligence springs a knowledge of moral truths and a correct vision of the function of political power as serving the interests of the governed. The interests of the state must have priority over the interests of any individual. Pericles had already expounded the idea that the interests of the individual citizen were best served by the success of the whole state. Thucydides has Pericles say:

> My own opinion is that when the whole state is on the right course it is a better thing for each separate individual than when private interests are satisfied but the state as a whole is going downhill. However well off a man may be in his private life, he will still be involved in the general ruin if his country is destroyed; whereas, so long as the state itself is secure, individuals have a much greater chance of recovering from their private misfortunes. (2.60)

In this view, harmony is the salvation of the state and the individual, while division fostered by the conflict of private interests with those of the state brings ruin. This is the central issue that Plato addresses in the *Republic* when he deals with the organization of the state.

Reading the Republic

Naturally, your primary task in studying the Republic is to learn and understand what Plato says in this work. But in order to derive the most benefit from reading the Republic, you must first put Plato's views in the context of what you have learned about Athens from tragedy, comedy, the Apology, and Thucydides. Plato's ideas do not exist in a historical vacuum; he was trying to deal with contemporary problems. Secondly, since Plato's views involve universal human concerns, which span the centuries between his time and ours, we should not hesitate to examine his ideas critically and measure them against our own experience, feelings, and common sense. Certainly it would violate the spirit of Socratic inquiry to accept uncritically everything that Plato says in the Republic. Although Plato was a brilliant philosopher and writer, and was able to identify the most significant problems of human existence, he was also a human being. His ideas are not always convincing nor even consistent; his arguments are not always supported by impeccable logic.

In reading the Republic, become actively engaged in the philosophic process. Imagine yourself as one of the interlocutors in the conversation led by Socrates at Cephalus's house. Examine Plato's ideas critically. Formulate questions about ideas which puzzle you. Try to answer them yourself, and bring them up in class for discussion. Even if a satisfactory answer can't be found, at least you've benefited from an active attempt to understand. Intellectual exercise of this kind can be quite rewarding.

Exercise for Reading Comprehension and Interpretation

Book 1. 327-47[4]

The dramatic setting of the Republic is the house of Cephalus, a wealthy businessman. His son Polemarchus has a prominent part in the opening portion of the dialogue after the departure of Cephalus. We know from a speech written by Polemarchus's brother, Lysias, that some seventeen years after the dramatic date[5] of this dialogue, during the rule of the Thirty, the wealth

---

[4] The numbers after the period refer to sections of the Republic. These numbers usually appear in the margins of the text (sometimes at the top of the page).

[5] The dramatic date of a literary composition is the time when the event described is supposed to have taken place as opposed to the actual date of composition.

of Polemarchus and Lysias, inherited from their father, attracted the attention of the Thirty, which resulted in the death of the former and the exile of the latter. Since the *Republic* was written well after these events, what view do you think Plato intends his reader to have of Cephalus's interest in the accumulation of wealth and his praise of its advantages (330-31)? What definition of justice does Socrates formulate based on the comments of Cephalus and how does he refute it (331)? Are telling the truth and paying what is owed just acts? If so, why is this definition of justice found inadequate?

Is Polemarchus's definition of justice, derived from the poet Simonides, an improvement over the preceding definition (332)? Explain your answer. How does Polemarchus's view of justice show that he is his father's son (333)? What problem does Socrates see in Polemarchus's definition of justice as helping one's friends and harming one's enemies (334)? Give one specific example of elenchus, involving a *reductio ad absurdum*,[6] that Socrates uses to demolish Polemarchus's definition of justice (334). How does Socrates define harm (334)? Why does he believe that it is never just to harm anyone (335)?

Why is Thrasymachus angry with Socrates (336-37)? What characteristic Socratic attitude and technique does he object to? What is Thrasymachus's definition of justice (338)? Explain the *reductio ad absurdum* used by Socrates in his refutation of this definition (339). What does Socrates' elenchus lead Thrasymachus to say is an essential qualification of the ruler (340-41)? What kind of analogies does Thrasymachus use to illustrate this point (340-41)? According to Socrates, what is the primary interest of any art and its practitioner? For example, what is the interest of the doctor and his art (342)?

According to Thrasymachus, what does his analogy of the herdsman prove about the main interest of the ruler (343)? What is his view of the comparative profitability of justice and injustice (343-44)? What is Socrates' view of this (344)? According to Socrates, what does the analogy of the shepherd prove about the proper interest of the ruler (345)? Why is wage-earning not the true and proper interest of any art (346)? Why would decent men in an ideal state be unwilling to rule (347)? Under what conditions would a man of integrity accept power (347)?

---

[6] *Reductio ad absurdum* is a technique of argument that disproves an hypothesis by pointing out the absurdity of its logical conclusion.

Book 2. 357-92

What are the three classes of good outlined by Glaucon (357)? In which class does Socrates place justice, and why does Glaucon disagree with this classification (358)? Explain how Glaucon will play the role of the devil's advocate in this section (358). What does he want to learn from Socrates about justice and injustice (358)? What view of justice does Glaucon as a devil's advocate present in his discourse on the social contract (359)? What does the story of Gyges seemingly illustrate about justice (359-60)? Why does Glaucon want to remove all considerations of reward from the analysis of justice and actually have the hypothetical just man suffer because of his justice (361)? According to Adeimantus, what arguments are usually put forward to children to convince them to be just (363)? What views of justice and injustice are presented by the poets (364)? What effect will these arguments and views have on young men (365)? What task does Adeimantus propose for Socrates (367)?

Where does Socrates propose to look for justice first? Why (368)? Why does a state come into existence in the first place (369)? What human needs are best satisfied by a state? Why is a state able to satisfy these needs better than any other manner of life (369)? Why ought a man keep to one occupation (370)? Where in the state are justice and injustice to be found (372)?

What problems does the introduction of luxuries cause for the hypothetical state under consideration (373)? Why is war the ultimate consequence of the luxurious state (373)? According to what principle is the army created (374)? Why does Socrates reject the notion of a citizen militia (374)?

What are the essential qualities that the Guardians[7] must possess (375-76)? Why is knowledge important (376)? Of what will the elementary intellectual education of the Guardians consist (377)? What objections does Socrates have to the stories told by Hesiod and Homer (377)? Why does he have these objections (378)? How can these stories be altered to become acceptable (379-80)? Identify what Socrates finds wrong with the following: the dream sent to Agamemnon by Zeus (382), myths about the underworld (387), the lamentations of Achilles and Priam (388), the laughter of the gods at Hephaestus (389), Achilles' threat to Apollo and dragging of Hector's body (391). How can deception be justified in certain circumstances (389)?

---

[7] The term *Guardians* is here used to refer to the army only. Later in the *Republic* this term will include both the rulers and the army. The latter will be specifically referred to as *Auxiliaries*.

Books 3. 414-16 and 4. 419-21

Plato[8] is fond of using myths of his own creation in his dialogues. In this section he presents two of these myths. The first myth recalls existing Greek stories of various peoples who have literally sprung from the earth of the area they inhabited. The second tells of men having different kinds of metals in their bodies and is apparently inspired by the metals in Hesiod's myth that characterize the various ages of mankind: gold, silver, bronze, and iron. As in the case of Hesiod's myth, Plato's story is clearly allegorical; that is, elements in the myth stand for something else beyond themselves.

Although Plato knows that these myths are not literally true, he believes that they are justified by serving a morally valid purpose in his ideal state (414). What do the different metals in Plato's myth represent? What purpose does each myth serve (414-15)?

What are the two primary duties of the Auxiliaries (415)? Why is the education of the Auxiliaries so important (416)? What kind of life is required of the Guardians (416-17)? Why does Plato require this life for the Guardians (416-17)? What objection does Adeimantus make to this life (419)? How does Socrates answer Adeimantus's objection (420)?

Book 4. 427-44

With reference to the state, what is wisdom, and who must possess this virtue (428)? Answer the same question with regard to courage and temperance (429-31). What then is justice with reference to the state (432-34)? Plato then moves to the question of justice in the individual. He assumes that there is no difference between a just man and a just society (435). Do you agree with this? Explain your answer. What parallelism does Plato believe exists between the state and the individual (435)? What are the three elements of the individual soul, and what is the nature of each element (439)? With which class in the state is each of these three elements linked (441)?

What are the true functions of each element of the soul (441)? Define the virtues of wisdom, courage, and temperance with reference to the soul (441-42). Define justice in the individual soul (443). What meaning does the metaphor of musical harmony have for justice (443)? How has justice been shown to be as obviously good for the individual as good health (444)?

[8] It is the general consensus that after Book 1, which presents Socrates in his historical role of using elenchus to point out the contradictions implicit in various definitions, he is being generally used as a mouthpiece for Plato's doctrines.

Books 6. 509-11 and 7. 514-21

In the "Divided Line" and "Allegory[9] of the Cave" Plato presents an illustration of his theory of knowledge. What does the unequal division of the Line and of each part of the Line (A-B, C-D), again in the same proportion, symbolize (509-10)? Through what means does one apprehend the world of appearances? the intelligible world? What is the crucial difference between the field of intelligible reality studied by dialectic and the subject matter of the sciences (511)?

The Allegory of the Cave is referred to by Plato as an *eikon*, "likeness," describing and commenting upon the human condition, its defects, and potentialities. Explain what each of the following elements in the story of the prisoners in the cave represents in Platonic philosophy: the prison, the prisoners, the shadows on wall, the escaped prisoner, the outside world and the Sun, the ascent from cave to upper world (517). Why is it worthwhile to achieve a knowledge of the Good (517)? Why are those who have gained this knowledge reluctant to become involved in the affairs of men (517)? What is the basic difference between justice in the real world and Justice itself (the essential Form of Justice) (517)? In Plato's view, what is education (518)? Why do some men of intelligence not achieve wisdom (519)? What special responsibility do men of wisdom have (520)? What is the only condition in which ideal government can exist (520)?

Book 8. 543-61

What determines the nature and quality of any government (544)? What begins the degeneration of the ideal government (546)? What is the character of the ruling class in a timocracy (547)? What kind of character does the timocrat have and on what does he base his claim to office (548-49)?

What qualifies a man for office in an oligarchy (550)? What is wrong with such a qualification in Plato's view (551)? What are the most serious defects of an oligarchy as a form of government (551-52)? What kind of character does the oligarchical man have (553-54)?

Why does an oligarchy degenerate into a democracy (555-57)? What are the most significant characteristics of a democracy (557-58)? What kind of character does the democratic man have (559-61)? What is wrong with the democratic man playing multiple roles in the state (561)?

---

[9] An allegory is a story in which characters, objects, and actions have metaphorical meaning.

Book 10. 613-20

The interpretation of the Myth of Er presents a difficulty. In the myth, rewards and punishments imposed by judges in an afterlife are presented as an encouragement to justice. Plato, previously in the *Republic*, had attempted to show that justice was worthwhile, both for its own sake and for the benefits that spring from its very nature, not because of consequences that are the result of someone else's judgment. For this and other reasons, Julia Annas has pointed out[10] that it is not clear whether we are to take the myth literally or look beyond the details of the narrative for a deeper message.

Who is Er? In what ways are the just and the unjust rewarded and punished (614-15)? For whom is an afterlife of punishment permanent (615)? Why? After a period of reward or punishment, what must the souls then do (617-18)? What life does the man who had drawn the first lot choose, and what consequences does this choice have (619)? Why does he make such a wrong choice (619)? What beneficial effect did the suffering in the earth experienced by some souls have for their choice of their next life (619)? What must the souls do before entering a new life (621)? What is the main lesson that the "Myth of Er" teaches (620)?

---

[10] *An Introduction to Plato's Republic* (Oxford: Oxford University Press, 1982), p. 353.

Apollo, the son of Zeus, who comes
to the defense of his priest, Chryses,
and favors the Trojans (*Iliad*).
Apollo is the source of prophecy at
Delphi in Sophocles's *Oedipus the
King* and in Plato's *Apology.*
Amphipolis, c. 390–357 B.C.

Philosophical Background of the Hellenistic Age

Hellenistic[1] philosophy, in contrast with the philosophy of Plato, which focused on the affairs of the polis, concentrated on the individual and his personal welfare. In general, Hellenistic philosophy recommended that the individual, in order to attain happiness, attempt to manage only what was for him personally manageable, his own character and thoughts. Man must become self-sufficient and not rely on anyone or anything outside himself for his well-being. Also, he must adopt an attitude toward external events that will result in attaining *ataraxia*, "imperturbability" (peace of mind), the goal of most Hellenistic philosophies.

In the Hellenistic period various philosophies were devised in order to help man achieve happiness. The most popular was Stoicism. The founder of Stoicism was a Cypriot named Zeno (335-263 B.C.), who came to Athens in 313 B.C. and taught in a public colonnaded hall called the *Stoa Poikile*, "Painted Porch," from which his philosophy acquired its name. The doctrines of Zeno's philosophy aimed at the typically Hellenistic ideals of peace of mind and self-sufficiency and viewed man first and foremost as a member of the human race and secondarily as a citizen of a particular polis.

Stoicism adopted a physical theory of the universe in part derived from that of the pre-Socratic Heraclitus. The basic stuff of the universe is not inert matter, but a living creative fire that contains the seeds of all creation. This fire pervades the whole universe in greater and smaller amounts. Higher forms of existence have more of it, while lower forms, less. In its purest form, it is identified with Reason and God, who is sometimes called Zeus. The existence of the other gods is not denied, but they are often interpreted symbolically as natural phenomena (for example, Apollo = the sun; Hera = air; Poseidon = the sea), or as human feelings (for example, Aphrodite = sexual urges). Although Stoicism uses the traditional names of the old anthropomorphic gods, its concept of divinity is entirely nonanthropomorphic.

The divine rational fire of the universe is also identified by the Stoics with Fate. Under the influence of Babylonian astrology, Stoicism adopted the idea of the sympathy of the universe. According to astrology, what happens

---

[1] The word *Hellenistic* comes from the verb *hellenizein*, which means "to speak Greek" and also "to Hellenize," that is, to make a non-Greek Greek. Because Alexander the Great had conquered the non-Greek East as far as India and had introduced Greek culture into that area, modern scholars have given the name Hellenistic to the period of Greek history and culture following his death in 323 B.C. and extending down to 146 B.C., when begins the period of Roman domination of Greece.

in one part of the universe affects what happens in another part. Man as a microcosm of the universe is affected by what happens in the heavens. This suited well the Stoic doctrine that man, whose soul consisted of a portion of the divine fire, was governed by the universal divine fire, which plotted out in advance human events. The most important difference between astrological fate and Stoic fate, however, is that the former is viewed pessimistically, while the latter is seen optimistically as a rational and providential principle. Stoic providential fate is best summed up in the modern saying: "Everything turns out for the best." Thus, human events that seem bad are only apparent evils; if the ultimate purposes of God were known, they would be seen as leading to some good. Man must learn to adjust to and accept what happens; to resist divine providence (that is, whatever happens) is wrong and useless. The only result of such resistance is loss of peace of mind. Willing cooperation with the Divine Will is the only sensible course of action and the essence of Stoic virtue.

The teachings of the early Stoics emphasized that man must learn to deal with whatever happens to him, whether good or bad, by eliminating such passions that disturb his soul as fear, greed, grief, and joy. He must attain a state of *apatheia*, "a complete lack of feeling," in order to achieve peace of mind. This unrealistic demand on human nature was characteristic of the extreme idealism of early Stoicism, which aimed at creating a limited utopian community of perfect wise men, who alone could achieve these high ideals. The Greek Stoic philosopher Panaetius (c.185-109 B.C.), however, made Stoicism a less exclusive philosophy, embracing the whole human race. He rejected the doctrine of *apatheia*, without diminishing the importance of self-control, and emphasized the equality and brotherhood of all men on the basis that every man's soul is derived from the divine rational fire. On a visit to Rome, Panaetius became friendly with Publius Scipio Aemilianus, the conqueror of Carthage, who was at the head of coterie of prominent philhellenic Romans, known today as the Scipionic Circle. In this way, the more humane values of Panaetius's version of Stoicism became popular among the Romans, who as a pragmatic people had little use for Greek philosophical idealism. Stoicism remained the dominant philosophy at Rome until the arrival of Christianity and even had a strong influence on the new religion.

Second only to Stoicism in popularity was the philosophy of Epicurus (341-270 B.C.), the son of an Athenian schoolteacher, who established his school at Athens in a garden attached to his house. For this reason Epicureanism was often referred to as the philosophy of the Garden. Epicurus's associates, including women and slaves, lived together in his house in a philosophical community, isolating themselves from civic affairs and sharing an almost ascetic way of life. Epicurus was a prolific writer, but most of his works are lost, including his major work *On Nature.*

Epicureanism shared with other Hellenistic philosophies the emphasis on the individual rather than the state, peace of mind, and self-sufficiency, but what set it apart was its common sense approach to life. Since man naturally seeks pleasure and avoids pain, Epicurus identified man's chief good as pleasure. This emphasis on pleasure earned Epicurus a bad reputation, both in ancient and modern times, that survives in the archaic meaning of the word *epicure* as a person devoted to the pleasures of the senses and to luxury. This is a misunderstanding of Epicurus's teachings. He saw pleasure as the absence of pain and pain as an unsatisfied desire for pleasure. But not every desire had to be satisfied. Epicurus divided bodily pleasures into three categories: physical and necessary (for example, food, drink, clothing, shelter); physical and not necessary (for example, sex); neither physical nor necessary (for example, luxurious clothing or any luxury): the first must be satisfied, the second must be enjoyed prudently, and the third must be avoided. Pain, therefore, will only result when desires for pleasures of the first category are not satisfied. But perhaps even more critical to human happiness, according to Epicurus, is the avoidance of mental pains, which typically ruin human happiness: anxiety caused by involvement in public affairs, remorse brought about by a guilty conscience, and the fear of the gods and of death. To avoid these pains is to experience pleasure of the mind and thus achieve *ataraxia.*

Epicurus supported his moral teachings with the physical theory of atomism, which he borrowed from the pre-Socratic philosopher Democritus of Abdera. His interest in atomism is not at all speculative, but quite pragmatic. Epicurus saw in atomism an explanation of the origin of the universe that eliminated the gods from the world[2] and proved that the soul was mortal. If man accepted atomism, then he would not be subject to those two great fears that are most destructive of human happiness: the fear of the gods and of punishment in the afterlife.

---

[2] But this is not to say that Epicurus was an atheist. He believed that the gods exist in the interspaces between the innumerable worlds and, because they have no involvement with the world and the troublesome life of mankind, are models of Epicurean *ataraxia.*

Poseidon, god of the sea.
Poseidonia, c. 510 B.C.

Epicurus takes a purely utilitarian view of virtue, which he sees as secondary in importance to the avoidance of pain. Any virtue that brings pain is not to be practiced. On the other hand, we can most often avoid serious mental pain by being virtuous, because when we do wrong, we are tortured by remorse. In Epicurean, ethics justice is not the all-encompassing moral principle presented by Plato, but a simple agreement among men not to harm or be harmed. In this light, justice is basically an effective means of diminishing the possibility of pain by agreeing not to inflict pain on others in return for not suffering pain.

Despite the Roman poet Lucretius's attempt in his poem *On the Nature of the Universe* to win his fellow citizens over to Epicureanism, this philosophy did not gain a large number of adherents at Rome. The Romans were a very religious people, and religion was an essential part of the political structure at Rome. The political process with its extensive use of augury[3] was predicated on the assumption that the gods were involved in the affairs of the Romans. The generally puritanical Romans also regarded with suspicion a philosophy that was so concerned with pleasure. Finally, Epicurus's recommendation of withdrawal from public life was not likely to earn his philosophy wide acceptance among an aristocracy that saw politics as a worthy and noble endeavor. With the advent of Christianity, Epicureanism met with even more hostility. Epicurus's teachings—that the soul is mortal, that the world is the result of a chance combination of atoms, that there is no providential god, and that the chief good is pleasure—were totally at odds with Christian doctrine.

---

[3] Augury is the practice of determining the will of the gods by observing and interpreting various omens (for example, the flight of birds).

Ancient Italy, Sicily, and Northern Africa

On the Nature of the Universe
Lucretius

Genre: Didactic Poetry

Lucretius's *On the Nature of the Universe* is an important example of a popular genre of ancient literature, didactic poetry. The purpose of this genre is to give instruction to the reader on various topics ranging from farming to philosophy. Lucretius's purpose is to explain Epicureanism to his readers and win them over as followers of this philosophy. Because of the scope of Lucretius's poem, which includes both the origin and dissolution of the universe, and also because of its meter (dactylic hexameter, as in the *Iliad*), it may be called an epic, but not in the same sense as the heroic narrative of Homer.

Historical Background

When Lucretius (*c*. 99-55 B.C.) wrote *On the Nature of the Universe*, Rome was experiencing political disorder. Political strife had begun in Rome in the late second century B.C. when attempts to enact land reform met with resistance from the Roman Senate, which resulted in the violent deaths of many advocates of agrarian legislation. From this time, Roman politicians were divided into two loosely organized parties: the *Populares*, Roman aristocrats who presented themselves as champions of the people, and the *Optimates*, aristocratic defenders of Senatorial authority. Early in the first century B.C., an attempt by the *Populares* to have Roman citizenship bestowed on Rome's Italian allies was met with violence, when the tribune who proposed discussion of this issue was murdered (91 B.C.). Soon afterwards, a dispute arose between two powerful Roman generals, Marius and Sulla. Marius, who on occasion sided with the *Populares*, and Sulla, a staunch defender of the Senate, came into conflict over an important command in the East. This strife resulted first in Sulla's taking Rome by force to obtain the command and then, after his departure to the East, the capture of Rome by Marius. Three years after Marius's death in 86 B.C., Sulla returned from the East and again used military force to gain the upper hand at Rome. Each victory by Marius or Sulla ended in the systematic murder of their political enemies. The final victory of Sulla was marked by an especially bloody massacre of his opponents. In 63 B.C., toward the end of Lucretius's life, a conspiracy to overthrow the Roman government was led by Catiline, a leader of the *Populares*. The attempt was defeated through the efforts of Cicero, the great Roman orator and consul of that year. Lucretius presents Epicureanism to his fellow Romans as an answer to how one can live a happy life in the midst of this political chaos.

Exercise in Reading Comprehension and Interpretation

Book 1. 1-482

Just as Homer begins his poems with an address to the Muse, Lucretius begins his poem with an invocation to the goddess Venus, the Roman counterpart of Aphrodite. Since it is a central doctrine of Epicureanism that the gods have no involvement with men, it is clear that Lucretius is addressing Venus as a symbolic figure. Read lines 1-40 carefully, and explain what Venus represents for Lucretius.

What great service did Epicurus do for man (62-79)? What does the example of Iphianassa illustrate (80-101)? What fears ruin man's happiness (102-11)? What special problem did Lucretius have in writing a Latin poem about Greek philosophy (136-39)?

According to Lucretius, what is the first principle of Nature (150)? What benefit does an understanding of this principle bring to man (151-58)? Give one argument that Lucretius uses to support this principle (159-214). What do all things require in order to come into existence (205-6)? What are all things made of (215-24)? Why must these basic elements of matter be indestructible (225-37)? Look up the modern scientific principle of conservation of mass in a good reference work. How do lines 262-64 (see 2. 303-7) represent this principle?

Give two arguments presented by Lucretius for the existence of atoms, despite their invisibility to the human eye (277-328). Why must empty space (the void) exist (329-45; 426-28)? Give two examples of void existing in created objects (346-69). What are the two basic mutually exclusive realities in the world (430-48)? Explain the difference between a property and an accident (449-58). Why are past events considered accidents of matter (459-82)?

Book 2. 1-477

According to lines 1-13, what should a man avoid in order to be happy? What general reference to contemporary events at Rome is evident in these lines? At what natural goal should our actions aim (14-21)? Are luxuries necessary for the enjoyment of pleasure (22-39)? Explain your answer. What is the best means of ridding oneself of superstitious fears (40-61)?

What are the two causes of the motions of atoms (83-85)? Why must atoms always be in motion (89-108)? What does the analogy of motes in a sunbeam illustrate (112-41)? Why does Lucretius believe that the universe was not made for man by the gods (167-81)? What is the natural movement of things having the property of weight (184-205)?

Why is the "swerve" necessary to allow for the possibility of creation (216-42)? Why is the swerve necessary for free will (251-93)? Look up the modern scientific principle of the conservation of energy in a good reference work. How do lines 297-99 represent this principle? What do the examples of grazing sheep and armies on maneuvers illustrate (308-32)? What do the various examples of different creatures and natural substances prove about atoms (333-97)? What is the reason for the differences in the tastes and smells of various natural substances (398-430)? What sense is the basis of all sensation (434-43)? What accounts for the hardness of some natural objects and the fluid nature of others (444-55)? How can a natural substance like sea-water be fluid and bitter at the same time (464-77)?

Book 3. 1-176; 830-1094

What kind of life do the gods lead as revealed by Epicurus to Lucretius (14-24)? Why do men cling to superstition (48-54)? What is the main reason men commit evil (59-93)? Explain your answer. Where is the mind located (139-40)? What kind of pain can the mind suffer (147-60)? How does Lucretius prove that the mind and spirit are corporeal (161-76)?

What benefits does death bring to us (830-930)? What lesson for man is evident in the simile of the banqueter (931-65)? Lucretius points out that although the traditional myths that tell of famous sinners being punished in the underworld are false, these sinners exist in this life figuratively in the persons of various human beings who suffer a hell on earth. Explain what Tantalus, Tityos, Sisyphus, and the Danaids each represent symbolically (978-1010). Why does belief in an afterlife of punishment destroy man's happiness (1014-23)? What are the examples of Ancus, Xerxes, Scipio, Homer, Democritus, and Epicurus meant to prove (1025-52)? What is the point of the example of the restless man (1053-75)? Why is our continual desire for new pleasures not a good reason for wanting to prolong our life (1076-94)?

Book 5. 783-1457

What is the origin of animals, birds, and the human race (783-825)? Why did many monsters created by the earth become extinct (837-56)? What qualities enabled other species to survive (862-77)? Look up Darwin's theories of natural selection and survival of the fittest in a good reference book, and compare them to the view presented in the last two passages. What are the similarities? Are there any differences? Why could the famous monsters of myth like the

Scylla and crab. Scylla, a sea
monster devours six of Odysseus's
crew (*Odyssey*).
Acragas, c. 420–415 B.C.

Centaur, Scylla, and the Chimaera never have existed (878-924)?

Describe briefly the life of primitive men (925-57). What kind of social organization did they have (958-65)? What were the pleasures and dangers of their life (966-98)? What advantages did they have over men of more advanced civilization (999-1010)? What was the result of men living in huts, wearing clothing, using fire, and the development of marriage and the family (1011-18)? What alliance did men finally establish (1019-20)? Why was this alliance necessary (1021-27)? Why was language invented (1028-32)? How did men discover fire (1091-1101)?

What kind of government was established first (1108-9)? What led to the elimination of this form of government (1120-42)? What kind of government replaced the first form and for what reason (1143-50)? How do violence and injury affect the wrongdoer (1151-60)? How does this argument illustrate the moral ideal of Epicurus?

In lines 1169-82, Lucretius refers to the process whereby men came to know of the gods' existence. The visions of the gods that men see when awake and in their sleep are not mere illusions, but the result of the material images that come off the bodies of the gods and enter the world from the interspaces between worlds where the gods live. In exactly the same way as objects in the world are perceived by men, the material images of the gods make contact with the atoms of the souls of men and thereby enable men to become aware of the gods' existence. According to Lucretius, the mistake that men make is to believe that the gods are involved in human affairs. Why did men create religion (1183-93)? How do men suffer needlessly because of their religious beliefs (1194-1240)? How does Lucretius define true piety (1202)?

The final section of the book (1241-1457) represents an attempt to demythologize the development of arts and crafts. In myth various gods were credited with the invention of these civilized techniques (for example, Hephaistos, metallurgy; Athene, weaving; Demeter, agriculture). According to Lucretius, how did men learn the process of metallurgy (1241-68)? What human endeavors encouraged progress in metallurgy (1281-96)? For what purpose were animals tamed (1297-1349)? What connection does weaving have with the use of iron (1350-53)? Why were men the first weavers (1356)? Why did they give up this task (1357-60)? How did men learn to practice agriculture (1361-69)? to sing and play the flute (1379-87)? to create a calendar (1436-39)? How do lines 1390-1411 represent a fulfillment of Epicurus's moral ideal? How do lines 1416-35 represent a violation of this ideal? By what general process did man learn arts and crafts (1448-57)? Explain how this explanation differs from the mythological point of view.

Heracles, the Greek hero and god who kills the monster Cacus, is a prototype of Aeneas and Augustus in Vergil's *Aeneid.*

Aeneid
Vergil

Genre: Literary Epic

Although the *Aeneid* shares many characteristics with the Homeric epic, it is different in important ways. The *Aeneid* is referred to as a literary or secondary epic in order to differentiate it from such primitive or primary epics as the Homeric poems. The terms *primitive, primary,* and *secondary* should not be interpreted as value judgments, but are merely indications that the original character of the epic was improvisational and oral, while the *Aeneid,* which came later in the epic tradition, was composed with the aid of writing. As we have seen, the Homeric poems give evidence of improvisational techniques of composition[1] involving the use of various formulas. This style of composition is suited to the demands of improvisation before an audience that do not allow the poet time to create new ways of expressing various ideas. In order to keep his performance going, he must depend upon stock phrases, which are designed to fill out various portions of the dactylic hexameter[2] line. Conversely, Vergil, composing in private, obviously spent much time creating his own personal poetic language. Thus, in reading the *Aeneid,* you will notice the absence of the continual repetition of formulas, which are unnecessary in a literary or secondary epic.

Vergil, however, does imitate Homeric language without the repetitions. This is another reason for calling the *Aeneid* a secondary epic. For example, Vergil occasionally translates individual Homeric formulas, or even creates such new formulas as "pious Aeneas" in imitation of Homer; he also imitates such other Homeric stylistic devices as the epic simile and uses the Homeric poems as a source for story patterns. Although in this sense the *Aeneid* can be called derivative, what Vergil has taken from Homer he has recast in a way that has made his borrowings thoroughly his own and Roman. For example, Vergil changed the value system characteristic of the Homeric epic, which celebrated heroic individualism, such as that displayed by Achilles in the *Iliad.* The heroic values of an Achilles would have been anachronistic and inappropriate in a poem written for Roman readers of the first century B.C., who required their leaders to live according to a more social ideal, suited to a sophisticated urban civilization. Therefore, although Vergil set the action of his poem in a legendary age contemporary with the Trojan War before

---

[1] It is not known for certain whether the Homeric poems were originally improvised, without the aid of writing, or were written down by the poet himself, or were dictated to a scribe and then recited, but it is clear that they were composed in the style of improvised oral poetry.
[2] In the *Aeneid,* Vergil uses this traditional meter of epic poetry.

Rome existed, one must judge the characters of his poem by the standards of the poet's own times.

Historical Background

Vergil (70-19 B.C.) lived through the politically violent and chaotic years of the failing Roman Republic, and his writings very clearly show the influence of the events of this period. Thus, an understanding of the history of this era is critical to the interpretation of the *Aeneid*.

After the powerful general Pompey returned from his extensive conquests in the East, in 62 B.C., the refusal of the Senate to approve his settlement of affairs there alienated him from the *Optimates*. As a result, he joined in political alliance with the leaders of the *Populares*,[3] Julius Caesar and Marcus Crassus. The alliance has come to be known as the First Triumvirate and was sealed by the marriage of Pompey to Caesar's daughter.[4] Employing the threat of Pompey's military power, these three men were able to impose their will on Rome. In this way Caesar insured his own election to the consulship in 59 B.C., and, in the following year, his assignment to the governorship of Gaul, which required the command of a large army to subdue the warlike natives. Caesar enjoyed great military successes against the Gauls for almost a ten-year period, but what meant most to him was the fact that he now had an army loyal to himself, making him equal to Pompey, who had for so long overshadowed him in military power.

In the late fifties, with Caesar in Gaul and Pompey virtually ruler at Rome, a split between the two leaders became increasingly evident, especially after the death of Caesar's daughter, which removed the last tie between them. Civil war was inevitable. As the poet Lucan put it: "Caesar is able to tolerate no man as his superior; Pompey, no man as his equal" (1. 125-26, translation by author). The war between Caesar and Pompey ended with the latter's defeat in Greece and assassination in Egypt. After his victory Caesar assumed the dictatorship at Rome, which ultimately was granted to him for life. Caesar was now sole ruler of Rome. Resentment at the loss of political freedom resulted in his assassination by Brutus, Cassius, and others in 44 B.C.

Caesar's army passed in good part into the possession of his eighteen-year-old grandnephew, Octavian, his chief heir, who was adopted as Caesar's

---

[3] For explanation of *Optimates* and *Populares*, see the Glossary.
[4] When Vergil has Anchises predict the civil war between these two leaders, their names are not mentioned, but they are referred to as father-in-law and son-in-law (6. 828-31).

son according to the terms of his will. Because of his youth, no one expected Octavian to be of any consequence in the political arena, but with a maturity beyond his years, he won over Caesar's veterans and was determined to avenge his adoptive father's death. Octavian came into immediate conflict with Caesar's lieutenant Antony, who felt that his close association with the dictator earned him the right to succeed Caesar. Cicero sided with Octavian and attacked Antony in a set of speeches called the *Philippics*, which resulted in Antony's being declared a public enemy. After Antony suffered a defeat at the hands of a coalition of military leaders (including Octavian), Antony and Octavian decided it would be in their own best interests to join in political alliance. They, along with Lepidus, formed the Second Triumvirate (43 B.C.) and ordered the execution of their political enemies. One of the most prominent victims was Cicero himself, whose death was demanded by Antony in revenge for the *Philippics* and was reluctantly agreed to by Octavian. At Antony's command Cicero's head and hands were cut off and placed on the speaker's platform in the Forum. This barbaric act serves as a vivid symbol of the bloody violence of the last years of the Republic.

Following the proscriptions, Antony and Octavian turned their attention to the assassins of Caesar and defeated them in Greece at the battle of Philippi (42 B.C.). Their alliance was weakened when Antony's brother revolted against Octavian while Antony was in Egypt, but was reconfirmed by the marriage of Antony and Octavian's sister, Octavia. There were two more temporarily successful attempts to prevent a split between Octavian and Antony, but Antony's romantic involvement with Cleopatra,[5] the queen of Egypt, which resulted in his rejection and ultimate divorce of Octavia, permanently alienated the two leaders. In addition, Antony's obvious intention to use the wealth of Egypt as a basis of power for uniting the East under his control made war unavoidable. The final conflict was a naval battle off Actium (31 B.C.) on the western coast of Greece, in which Antony and Cleopatra were routed by Octavian's fleet. The defeated pair later committed suicide in Alexandria.

After Actium, Octavian embarked on a program of restoring order and of reestablishing Rome's moral and religious traditions. He made a show of

[5] Cleopatra was a member of the Ptolemies, the Greek ruling family of Egypt, which had controlled Egypt since the death of Alexander. As was the custom, she was married to her brother Ptolemy XIII, and after his death, to another brother, Ptolemy XIV. During his campaign in the East, after his victory over Pompey, Julius Caesar had a love affair with her and fathered a son.

restoring the free Republic, but Octavian, with his control over the Roman army and finances, was in fact the sole ruler of Rome and its empire. In 27 B.C. the Roman Senate bestowed upon him the honorific title of Augustus,[6] which symbolized his special position of authority in the state. Octavian was welcomed as a savior by such writers as Vergil and Horace, the great lyric poet, and by the vast majority of Romans, because he had brought peace to Rome after a century of civil conflict. The admiration expressed by the poets for Octavian's accomplishments, although its effusiveness is sometimes offensive to modern taste, should not be interpreted as mere servile praise and political propaganda, but as an honest appreciation of a political leader who had brought an end to the horrors of civil war and was able to act with moderation after his victory.

Reading the Aeneid

The *Aeneid* differs from the *Iliad* and the *Odyssey* in that it often gives evidence of meaning beyond the narrative level. Homeric narrative is fairly straightforward; there is generally no need to look for significance that is not explicit in the story. On the other hand, although Vergilian narrative can be read and enjoyed as a story, it is often densely packed with implicit symbolic meaning. Frequently the implicit reference is to Roman history. While Homer is little concerned with the relationship of the past to the present—the past is preserved for its intrinsic interest as a story—Vergil recounts the legend of Aeneas because he believes it has meaning for Roman history and especially for his own times. For example, the destruction of Troy, resulting in Aeneas and his followers wandering west to find a new life, can be seen as parallel to the history of Rome in the first century B.C., which included both the violent destruction of the Republic and the creation of peace and order by Augustus. Also suggestive of the Roman civil wars is the civil war between the Trojans and their Italian allies, and Aeneas's victory over the Italians in this war suggests Augustus's ending of the Roman civil wars. The Carthaginian queen Dido, whose beauty almost makes Aeneas forget his duty as a leader, reminds the reader of Cleopatra's similar relationship with Antony. Dido's story also provides a legendary explanation for the historical hostility between Rome and Carthage that resulted in three wars. These are only a few examples of the importance of Roman history in the *Aeneid*. In the questions at the

[6] The title *Augustus* had special religious associations and was etymologically related to the Latin word *auctoritas*, "authority."

end of this section, help will be provided to enable you to see other implicit allusions to Roman history.

Another important difference between the *Aeneid* and the Homeric poems is that the former has a philosophical basis, while the latter were composed in an era completely innocent of philosophy. The *Aeneid* gives evidence of the influence of Stoicism, a Hellenistic philosophy that had gained many adherents in the Greek world and, by the first century B.C., had become the most popular philosophy of the educated classes at Rome. In reading the *Aeneid* be alert for Stoic influence. Note the connection between fate and the foundation of Rome. Also note when Aeneas adheres to Stoic ethical principles[7] and when he does not. Finally, be sure to read carefully Anchises' digression on the nature of the universe and human existence (6. 724-51), which combines Stoic physical theory with Orphic and Pythagorean teachings (reincarnation; see the Myth of Er in Plato's *Republic*). On the other hand, the gods in the *Aeneid*, for the most part, do not reflect the Stoic view of divinity. They are basically the traditional anthropomorphic deities of myth as required by the conventions of epic. On occasion, however, Stoic influence is evident, as in Book 1, when Jupiter is closely identified with providential fate (1. 262 ff.).

Another important aspect of the interpretation of the *Aeneid* is Vergil's use of the Homeric poems. In the *Aeneid* there are innumerable echoes of the *Iliad* and the *Odyssey*. Do not be concerned if you do not immediately recognize the allusions to Homer; it takes some experience and practice. Some echoes are so subtle that they go unnoticed even by experienced readers of the poem. Perhaps the most important connections for you to make will be in Book 12, where your knowledge of the *Iliad* will enable you to see how important figures of Vergil's poem are associated in various ways with heroes of the *Iliad*. Once these connections are identified, you will see that these references to the *Iliad* provide an interesting and significant commentary on the action of the *Aeneid*.

Finally, you should be conscious of such recurring images in the *Aeneid* as snakes, wounds, fire, hunting, and storms, and their meaning for the narrative. In your study of the imagery, notice the Vergilian technique of making a real part of the story an image and vice-versa. For example, consider hunting in the *Aeneid*. In Book 1, Aeneas is a real hunter who slays deer;

---

[7] See "The Philosophical Background of the Hellenistic Age," p. 116.

in Book 4, in a simile, he is a metaphorical hunter of Dido, and then again, a real hunter as he and Dido engage in a hunting expedition. No doubt Vergil intended these three instances of hunting to refer to each other implicitly and to comment upon the story. Recurring words also have a significance in the *Aeneid*. This is different, however, from word repetitions in the Homeric poems, which, due to the nature of oral poetry, regularly employ constant repetition of formulas for the sake of meter. Of course, recurring words in the *Aeneid* are not always obvious to the reader in translation, since translators do not translate any given Latin word in the same way every time; but even if there is not consistent translation of a given Latin word, the concepts that these recurring words convey can be identified in translation. Two of the most important recurrent words in the *Aeneid* are *furor*—which means "violent madness," "frenzy," "fury," or "passionate desire"—and its associated verb, *furere*, "to rage," "to have a mad passion." These words have important meaning for the characters in the *Aeneid* to whom they are applied and whose behavior must be evaluated by reference to the Stoic ethical ideal. In addition, these two words connect the legendary world of the *Aeneid* with Roman politics of the first century B.C., because they were often used in prose of the late Republic to describe the political chaos of that era.

In reading the *Aeneid*, try to be aware of such interpretive points as those described above. With attention to these details of interpretation you will begin to appreciate the art of Vergil and better understand the meaning of the poem.

Exercise in Reading Comprehension and Interpretation

Book 1

Just as Homer used the first lines of the *Iliad* and *Odyssey* to announce the main themes of those poems, Vergil presents the two main themes of the *Aeneid* in the first line. What are these two central themes? What universal force is responsible for Aeneas's sufferings as an exile (2[8])? In accordance with this universal force, what is the purpose of his sufferings (5-7)?

---

[8] The numbers in parentheses refer to line numbers in the *Aeneid*.

Explain the reasons for Juno's hatred of the Trojans (12-33). Why is it appropriate to Juno's character that she uses a storm to keep Aeneas away from Italy (50 ff.)? What do you think the storm represents symbolically? Aeneas's speech during the storm at sea is an adaptation of a speech of Odysseus in the *Odyssey*. Odysseus, also in the process of being shipwrecked, says:

> Three and four times blessed are the Danaans who perished
> in broad Troy bringing favor to the sons of Atreus.
> How I wish I had died and met my fate
> on that day when innumerable Trojans threw their bronze-tipped spears
> at me around the corpse of Peleus's son.
> I would have received my funeral honors and the Achaians would remember
>   my glory.
> Now it is my fate to die a pitiful death. (*Odyssey* 5. 306-12, translation by author)

What does Aeneas's similar speech tells us about his character (94-101)? Compare his speech with that of Odysseus. What is the most important difference? Compare the beginning of the action of the *Aeneid* with that of the *Iliad*. Does Vergil imitate Homer's *in medias res* beginning? Explain your answer.

The first simile in the poem is an extended simile that describes Neptune's calming of the storm (148-56). How does this simile connect the narrative of the *Aeneid* with first century B.C. Rome? What is the cause of violence in the simile (150)? Do you find any similarity between this cause and the cause of the storm? Explain your answer.

What is the purpose of Aeneas's hunting (180 ff.)? What does Aeneas's speech tell us about his character (198-207)? Why does Venus make a complaint to Jupiter (229-53)? Sum up in one sentence the essence of Jupiter's reply (257-96). The Julius Caesar mentioned by Jupiter (286-88) is in fact Augustus, who was legally entitled to use his adoptive father's name. Describe the result of his dominion according to Vergil (291-96). Note the personification of Sacrilegious Fury (*Furor impius*), which is a negation of those values that Aeneas is supposed to represent. *Furor* is opposed to the rational control of one's passions and acceptance of fate, while *impius* involves a repudiation of *pietas*, "devotion to one's gods, country and parents," which is the characteristic virtue of Aeneas. What benefit does the imprisonment of Sacrilegious Fury bring to Rome?

What is especially ironical about Venus wearing a disguise that would allow her to resemble a Spartan maiden or the virgin goddess Diana, sister of Apollo (315-16; 329)? Sum up in one sentence the information that Venus gives Aeneas (335-70). Why is Venus in disguise when she gives this information to her son (compare her later order that Cupid assume a disguise, 684)? What event does Aeneas see depicted on the walls of Dido's temple (453-93)? What is Aeneas's reaction to these scenes (462-65)? Why does he react in this way? The last figure depicted before the appearance of Dido is the Amazon queen Penthesilea, who near the end of the war came as an ally to Troy and was killed by Achilles (490-93). In what way could Vergil's description of Penthesilea be said to apply to Dido? When she appears, Dido is immediately compared to Diana (498-502). What is the purpose of this simile? Can you suggest any other meaning implicit in this comparison beyond mere description?

What is Dido's first reaction to Aeneas (613-30)? What trick does Venus plan (657-88)? Why does Venus believe that this trick is necessary (661-62)? What literary device is Vergil employing in line 712? What request does Dido make of Aeneas at the banquet (753-56)?

Book 2

What trick did the Greeks prepare for the Trojans (13-39)? Why didn't the Trojans believe Laocoön's warning and the evidence of their own ears (54)? Why do the Trojans believe Sinon's false story (145)? What is the fate of Laocoön (199-227)? What is the reaction of the Trojans to this event (228-49)? What literary device is Vergil employing in lines 238-40?

What advice does the ghost of Hector give to Aeneas (289-95)? How does Aeneas react to the attack on Troy (314-17)? Does Aeneas view his behavior on that night in a positive or negative light? Explain your answer. Note the snake imagery in the two similes (379-81; 471-75). In conjunction with the appearance of the twin snakes in the Laocoön incident, what meaning does this snake imagery suggest?

It has been suggested that Vergil's description of Priam's corpse (557-58) was inspired by a contemporary account of Pompey's death, of which we have a version in Plutarch's *Life of Pompey*: "They [Pompey's assassins] cut off Pompey's head and threw the rest of his body, naked, out of the boat, leaving it there [on the shore] as a spectacle for those who desired to see such a sight"[9] (80). What meaning is Vergil suggesting by describing the corpse of Priam in such a way as to recall Pompey?

[9] Translation by R. Warner, *Fall of the Roman Republic* (New York: Penguin, 1972), p. 241.

What is Aeneas's reaction to the sight of Helen (567-87)? What arguments does Venus use to convince Aeneas not to kill Helen (594-620)? What is Anchises' reaction to Aeneas's desire to save him (641-49)? What changes Anchises' mind (682-700)? Describe the manner in which Aeneas, his father, and son leave Troy (707-25). What symbolism is suggested by this scene? What is the fate of Aeneas's wife Creusa (737-40)? What advice does the ghost of Creusa give to Aeneas (776-89)?

Book 4

In the first two lines, the two dominant images of the book are introduced. What are they and to what do they refer? Be alert for their appearances throughout the book. Try to determine what comment they make on Dido and her fate.

What effect has Aeneas had on Dido (9-23)? Why was Dido determined to remain unmarried (15-29)? What advice does Anna give Dido (31-53)? Analyze carefully the simile in lines 69-73. What meaning does this simile have for the story? What effect does her passion have on Dido (76-89)?

What suggestion does Juno make to Venus (93-104)? What is Venus's reaction to this suggestion (105-14)? How does Juno propose to accomplish her plan (115-27)? How does Venus react to this plan (127-28)? Why does Vergil have Juno choose the occasion of a hunt for the consummation of the love affair (compare the hunting simile in lines 69-73 and the wound imagery of the whole book)? What comment is made about this love affair by the simile comparing Aeneas to Apollo in lines 143-49 (compare the simile in Book 1. 498-502 comparing Dido to Diana)? What literary device is Vergil employing in lines 169-70?

How do the peoples of Libya find out about the love affair (173-88)? Find an example of personification in this passage. Who is Iarbas? What prayer does he make to Jupiter (206-18)? How does Jupiter answer his prayer (223-37)? What is Aeneas's reaction to Mercury's message (279-95)? What comment does the simile in lines 300-4 make on Dido's behavior when she discovers that Aeneas is about to leave her? What complaints does Dido make to Aeneas (305-30)? How does Aeneas answer Dido (333-61)? What hope does Dido express and what threat does she make (382-87)? What specific philosophy seems to be implicit in Dido's words in lines 379-80 with regard to her view of the gods?

Analyze carefully the passage that contains the oak tree simile (438-49). What kind of heroism does Aeneas display at this moment? Is this the kind

of heroism generally exhibited by a Homeric hero (for example, Achilles)?
Explain your answer. Measure Aeneas's behavior here against the Stoic ethical
ideal.

Describe Dido's condition after Aeneas's final rejection (465-74). Measure her behavior against the Stoic ethical ideal. What does she resolve to
do (475-77)? How does she conceal her plan from Anna (478-98)? Why does
she think that her plan is her only possible course of action (534-52)? What
reference to Roman history does the final part of Dido's curse contain (622-29)?
Explain how the two dominant images of the book become real elements
in the narrative at the end of Book 4 and the beginning of Book 5 (1-5).
Explain why Dido is considered a tragic figure.

Book 6

At the invitation of his father's ghost (5. 724-39), Aeneas visits the underworld. Aeneas's trip to the land of the dead is modeled on Odysseus's visit
to the same place in Book 11 of the *Odyssey*. In both cases the purpose of
the trip to the underworld is the quest for knowledge only obtainable from
the dead. Odysseus gets his information from Teiresias; Aeneas, from his father,
Anchises.

Aeneas enters the underworld at the temple of Apollo at Cumae, in
southern Italy. He is accompanied by the god's priestess, the Sibyl. What
prophecy does the Sibyl make to Aeneas (83-97)? How do the details of her
prophecy resemble the circumstances of the Trojan War? What does the Sibyl
tell Aeneas he must do in order to enter the land of the dead (133-55)? How
does the mistletoe simile (205-7) symbolically point out the appropriateness
of the golden bough as a token necessary for entrance to the underworld?

How are ghosts transported across the river Styx (299-304)? Why are
some spirits not allowed to cross the river Styx (322-30)? Whom does Aeneas
meet among these ghosts, and what request does he make of Aeneas (337-71)?
How does Aeneas respond to this request (373-81)?

In the Mourning Fields, Aeneas meets the ghost of Dido (440-76). This
meeting recalls a passage in the *Odyssey* (11. 541-67), in which Odysseus
encounters Aias, son of Telamon, in the underworld. Aias—whose suicide
has been motivated by his shame at losing to Odysseus a contest for the arms
of Achilles—reacted with hostile silence to Odysseus's friendly overtures in
the underworld. How does Dido react to Aeneas's apologetic words (469-74)?

In the area reserved for famous military heroes Aeneas meets Deiphobus
(477-547). Who is Deiphobus and what was his fate on Troy's last night?

What area is reserved for the punishment of the wicked (548-58)? for the reward of the good (638-44)? What kind of goodness is required for entrance into this area (660-64)?

What information does Anchises want to convey to Aeneas, and what does he hope to achieve by summoning Aeneas to the underworld (713-18)? What does Aeneas's comment on the souls awaiting return to life indicate about his state of mind at this point (719-21)? In lines 724-51, Anchises gives Aeneas an account of the purification of souls and reincarnation. The passage, in general, combines Stoic theory with Orphic and Pythagorean doctrines found in Plato's Myth of Er. In Vergil's day these Greek teachings had become a part of Roman Stoicism. What is specifically Stoic about the view of emotions presented in the first part of Anchises' account (732-38)? Strict Stoic theory rejected the existence of reward and punishment in the afterlife, but taught that the soul went through a process of purgation until it was pure enough to rejoin the divine fire from which it sprang. According to Anchises, by what means is purgation of the soul accomplished (739-42)?

In lines 756-885, Aeneas sees the future of Rome in the form of the souls of famous Roman leaders from the time of the foundation of the city to Vergil's own day. In their midst is Augustus Caesar (789-805). What achievements are prophesied for Augustus? How do the comparisons with Hercules and Bacchus emphasize these achievements? What role in history does Anchises assign to the Romans (847-53)? To whom are the Romans implicitly compared in this passage?

Despite the general optimism of Anchises' review of the Roman future, his listing of great Roman heroes ends on a tragic note with Marcellus, Augustus's nephew and designated heir, who died at a young age (860-85). As will be evident later in the poem, in the case of Pallas and others, Vergil is much moved by youthful death. He sees it as one of the unfortunate tragedies required by providential fate in the accomplishment of destiny.

The book ends with Aeneas's return to the upper world through the ivory gate. What usually goes up to the world through this gate (895-96)? These two lines have been much debated throughout the history of Vergilian scholarship. What comment do you think Vergil is making here on Aeneas's trip to the underworld?

Book 8

What advice does the river god Tiber give to Aeneas (36-65)? Aeneas arrives at the future site of Rome and is greeted by Pallas and his father Evander, who dwell on the Palatine Hill, where Augustus later had his house.[10] Evander tells the story of Hercules' defeat of the primitive fire-breathing monster, Cacus, which is the reason for the celebration of rites at this site in honor of Hercules (185-267). Hercules was a prototypical Stoic hero, who was credited with bringing justice and peace to the world by his labors on behalf of civilization and consequently was made a god for his efforts. In Book 1 (289-90), Jupiter predicted that Augustus would become a god. In Book 6 (801-3), Augustus was compared favorably with Hercules. If Hercules is a prototype of Augustus, what meaning does the story of Cacus add to Vergil's view of Augustus? Hercules also serves as a prototype of Aeneas. What do the two heroes have in common (288-302)?

What request does Venus make of Vulcan (374-86)? What is his answer (395-404)? What scene in the *Iliad* is this meant to recall (see *Iliad* 18. 368 ff.)?

Why does Evander urge Aeneas to seek the aid of Etruria (470-509)? What help does Evander give Aeneas (514-19)?

State in general terms what is depicted on Aeneas's shield (626-28). Note especially the depiction of the battle of Actium and Augustus's triumph (675-728). Why does the battle of Actium occupy a central position (675) on the shield? What view does Vergil present of Antony and Cleopatra (685-88; 696-97; 707-8)? of the conflict between Egyptian and Roman gods (698-713)? What earlier event in the poem do the twin snakes recall (697)? What effect does the intervention of Apollo (Augustus's patron divinity) have (704-6)?

Book 12

Analyze carefully the simile in lines 4-8. What earlier character in the poem is suggested by the first two lines of the simile? Explain your answer. The words "with bloody mouth" recall the description of personified *Furor* (1. 294-96). What is the significance of these reminiscences with reference to the character of Turnus? Turnus accepts the idea of single combat with Aeneas to determine the outcome of the war, but both King Latinus and Queen Amata try to dissuade him (10-63). Identify the Iliadic allusion in this passage (see *Iliad* 22. 38-89).

After Aeneas agrees to a truce for the purpose of the duel (111-12), what information does Juno give to and what request does she make of Turnus's

---

[10] Vergil's description of Evander's house as small (366) is no doubt meant to make his readers think of Augustus's modest house on the Palatine.

sister Juturna (142-59)? For Iliadic parallel, see *Iliad*, Book 4, lines 68-72. How does Juturna go about carrying out this request (222-65)? What happens to Aeneas (318-23)? For the Iliadic parallel, see *Iliad*, Book 4, lines 124-40. With what hero of the *Iliad* is Aeneas identified by means of this Homeric echo? What is the significance of this identification for the *Aeneid*? Compare the reactions of Aeneas and Turnus to the breaking of the truce (313-17; 324-30). How is Aeneas's attitude different in lines 565-73?

Why does Amata commit suicide (593-603)? Describe her state of mind. What is the Iliadic parallel for Turnus's words in lines 643-45 (see *Iliad* 22. 99-103)? What is the significance of this parallel for Turnus? What is Turnus's attitude toward his final battle with Aeneas (676-80)? What comment does the simile in lines 684-89 make upon Turnus? For the Iliadic parallel, see *Iliad*, Book 13, lines 137-42. Identify the Iliadic allusions for lines 725-27, 763-65 and 908-12 (see *Iliad* 22. 209-13; 158-61; 199-201), and explain their significance for Turnus and Aeneas.

How does Juno answer Jupiter's request that she give up her resistance to fate (808-28)? What is Jupiter's reaction to her answer (830-40)? What sign does Jupiter give to Turnus and Juturna (843-71)? What does this omen mean (874-86)? What is the Iliadic parallel for Turnus's suppliancy to Aeneas in lines 931-38 (see *Iliad* 22. 250-59; 338-43)? With what Iliadic heroes are Aeneas and Turnus identified by means of the various Homeric echoes throughout the last half of Book 12? What is the significance of these identifications? What is Aeneas's first reaction to Turnus's suppliancy (938-41)? Why does Aeneas kill Turnus (941-49)? What comment does line 946 make on the character of Aeneas at this point? How would you evaluate Aeneas's action in the light of the Stoic ethical ideal? Why do you think Vergil ended the poem in this way?

Labyrinth. A maze built by
Daedalus as a prison for the
Minotaur. Theseus finds his way
into the building with Ariadne's
help (*Aeneid*).
Cnossus, c. 350–325 B.C.

Writing a Core Studies 1 Paper

Having to write a paper for a college course is often a frightening prospect for a student. Indeed, the process of expressing one's thoughts logically in written form can be difficult even for an experienced writer, but by avoiding certain pitfalls, you can improve your chances of doing well in the Core Studies 1 writing assignments Here is some general advice about writing papers for this course.

First, be sure that you understand what is required by your teacher. If you are confused in any way about the assignment, it is a good idea to meet with your teacher to discuss exactly what is expected. Misunderstanding of the assignment can only result in wasted effort and a low grade.

Once you have the assignment clear in your mind, read carefully the ancient text(s) involved in your topic. As you read, identify passages relevant to your topic and begin to form the ideas that will be the nucleus of your paper. Students sometimes lack confidence in their ability to make judgments based on evidence from a text, but this is exactly what you are trying to learn in Core Studies 1. Don't be afraid to rely on your own ideas. Generally, it is not necessary to consult secondary works (modern books and articles written about ancient texts and ancient life), unless your teacher specifies otherwise. However, if you do paraphrase or quote from a secondary work (or even from an ancient text), identify the source for your reader. Be sure that every direct quotation is surrounded by quotation marks. To pass someone else's words and/or ideas off as your own, either intentionally or even unintentionally, is *plagiarism*, the worst offense a writer can commit.[1]

The next step is to develop a thesis: a main idea that is the focus of your paper. Evaluate every statement that you include in your paper with regard to its logical connection with your thesis. This is the only way your paper can have those two essential qualities of good writing: unity and coherence.

After you have finished your first draft, put your paper aside for a time, anywhere from a few hours to a full day, and then begin to revise. In this way, you can read your own work with a fresh and more critical point of view. The most important part of the process of revision is a critical evaluation of the logical organization of your paper. Do your ideas really make sense? Does every statement in your paper contribute to the proof of your thesis?

Consult a text like *The Little, Brown Handbook* on the topics of plagiarism and paraphrase.

Revision also involves proofreading for mistakes in spelling[2], grammar, and punctuation. Carelessness in these matters detracts from a paper even though it may contain good ideas. Revision is as important as the writing of your first draft. That's why it's a serious mistake to wait until the last minute to do a writing assignment. If you are rushing to meet a deadline, you are likely to neglect this vital process. Be sure to allow sufficient time for revision.[3]

Finally, when your paper is returned to you with the teacher's comments, don't just look at the grade and put the paper out of your mind. Accept any criticism with a positive attitude; writers who want to improve must be willing to accept and learn from negative comments about their work. An excellent practice is to rewrite your paper in light of your teacher's criticisms. Ask your teacher to read the rewritten paper to see if it is an improvement over the first version. Perhaps your teacher will even allow you to submit the rewritten paper for a higher grade. Even if not, you cannot help but profit from the invaluable exercise of thinking logically in written form.

---

[2] Especially be sure that names of works, characters, and places are spelled correctly. It is very annoying to the teacher grading papers to see names constantly misspelled, when the student could have easily checked the correct spelling in the text. Negligence in this area can hurt your grade.

[3] For a fuller discussion of revision, consult a text like *The Little, Brown Handbook*.

Persephone, a goddess of the
underworld, daughter of Demeter
and Zeus.
Siculo-Punic, c. 270–260 B.C.

Chronological Table

Greece	B.C.	Rome
Mycenean Greeks control Aegean and Mediterranean areas	*c.* 1500–1100	
Fall of Troy	*c.* 1200	
Fall of Mycenae	*c.* 1100	
Dark Ages of Greece	*c.* 1100–750	
Ionian migrations to Asia Minor	*c.* 1000	
First celebration of Olympic Games	776	
	753	Traditional date of the founding of Rome
Phoenician alphabet adopted and adapted by Greeks	Late 8th century	
Homer		
Hesiod		
Greek colonization of the Mediterranean, Black Sea, Eastern Sicily, and Southern Italy	750–550	
Lyric Age of Greece	7th & 6th centuries	
Ionian Philosophy	6th & 5th centuries	
Aeschylus (525–456)		
Sophocles (c. 496–406)	509	End of Roman monarchy; Rome becomes a republic
First Persian War: Battle of Marathon	490	
Second Persian War: Battles of Thermopylae, Salamis, and Plataea	480–479	

Greece		Rome
Herodotus (c. 480–425)		
Euripides (c. 480–406)		
Delian League established	477	
Socrates (469–399)		
Thucydides (c. 460–400)		
Democritus (c. 460–?)		
Aristophanes (c. 448–385)		
Peloponnesian War	431–404	
Plague at Athens	430	
Death of Pericles	429	
Plato (c. 429–347)		
Mytilenian Debate	428	
Revolution at Corcyra	427	
Melian Affair	416	
Sicilian Expedition	415–413	
Fall of Athens	404	
Aristotle (384–322)		
Demosthenes (384–322)		
Epicurus (341–270)		
Philip of Macedon conquers Greece in Battle of Chaeronea	338	
Reign of Alexander the Great; beginning of Hellenistic culture	336–323	
Zeno, Stoic (335–263)		
	264–241	First Punic War: Sicily becomes a Roman province
		Plautus (c. 254–184)

Greece   **Rome**

218–201	Second Punic War: Hannibal invades Italy
200–100	Parts of Greece, Spain, North Africa, Asia Minor, and Gaul become Roman provinces
149–146	Third Punic War: Rome destroys Carthage
146	Greece becomes a Roman province
133–123	Tribunate of Tiberius (133) and tribunate of Gaius Gracchus (123): beginning of the Roman revolution
	Cicero (106–43)
	Caesar (102–44)
	Lucretius (c. 99–55)
88–82	Civil war: Marius and Sulla
	Vergil (70–19)
	Horace (65–8)
63	Cicero's consulship: Catiline's conspiracy defeated
60	First Triumvirate: Caesar, Pompey, and Crassus
58–51	Caesar's conquest of Gaul and invasion of Britain
49–48	Civil war between Caesar and Pompey
48	Battle of Pharsalus: Caesar defeats Pompey; Pompey assassinated in Egypt
46–44	Caesar dictator
44	Caesar assassinated

Greece		Rome
	43	Second Triumvirate: Octavian, Antony, and Lepidus
	42	Battle of Philippi: Antony and Octavian defeat Brutus and Cassius
	31	Battle of Actium: Octavian defeats Antony and Cleopatra
	27	Octavian given honorific title of Augustus

Glossary

Achaians (also spelled *Achaeans*), name used by Homer for the Greeks (also called Danaans and Argives).

Achilleus (also spelled *Akhilleus* and *Achilles*), hero of the *Iliad*.

Actium, a promontory on the northwestern coast of Greece, off which Octavian defeated Antony and Cleopatra in a naval battle, 31 B.C. (*Aeneid*).

Adeimantus, a brother of Plato and one of the interlocutors in the *Republic*.

Aeneas, hero of the *Aeneid*.

Aeschylus, earliest of the three great Athenian tragedians.

Agamemnon, leader of Greek expedition against Troy (*Iliad*).

Agave, mother of Pentheus (*Bacchae*).

Aias (son of Telamon), second greatest warrior of the Greeks at Troy and member of the embassy to Achilleus in the *Iliad*.

Alcibiades, a friend of Socrates and a general of the Athenian expedition against Sicily, who, when charged with impiety, went over to the Spartans (Thucydides).

Alexander the Great, Macedonian king who by conquest brought Greek civilization to the East as far as India.

Alexandros, see *Paris*.

Allegory, a story in which characters, objects, and actions have metaphorical meaning.

Amata, Latin queen who favors Turnus over Aeneas as her son-in-law (*Aeneid*).

Anagnorisis (variously translated as *discovery* or *recognition*), an important element of tragedy, according to Aristotle's *Poetics*, whereby a tragic protagonist gains information, previously unknown, leading to important insight.

Anaxagoras of Clazomenae, pre-Socratic philosopher and friend of Pericles, indicted by the Athenians for impiety; mentioned by Socrates in the *Apology*.

Anchises, father of Aeneas (*Aeneid*).

Andromache, wife of Hektor (*Iliad*).

Anna, Dido's sister (*Aeneid*).

Anthropomorphism, attribution of human form and behavior to the gods.

Antigone, heroine of the *Antigone*.

Antony, Roman general defeated by Octavian in the battle of Actium (*Aeneid*).

Anytus, leader of democratic exiles against the Thirty and one of Socrates' accusers in the *Apology*.

Apatheia, a lack of feeling; the Stoic doctrine that man must learn to ignore passions (fear, greed, grief, joy) that disturb his peace of mind.

Aphrodite, goddess of love, who favors Paris (*Iliad*).

Apollo, god who comes to the defense of his priest Chryses and favors the Trojans (*Iliad*), and who is also the source of prophecy at Delphi (*Oedipus the King* and *Apology*).

Apology, in a literary sense, a formal statement of justification or defense, such as Plato's *Apology*.

Arete, excellence.

Argeiphontes, see *Hermes*.

Argives, see *Achaians*.

Aristophanes, Athenian comic playwright.

Aristotle, philosopher, student of Plato, and tutor of Alexander the Great; author of the *Poetics*.

Ascanius, son of Aeneas, also known as Iulus, a name that designates him as an ancestor of the Julian family at Rome (*Aeneid*).

Ataraxia, calmness of mind; ideal state of mind sought by Hellenistic philosophies.

Athene, goddess who favors Achilleus and the Achaians in the Trojan War (*Iliad*).

Atomism, theory originated by Leucippus, developed by Democritus, and adopted by Epicurus as a basis of his moral philosophy, according to which the universe is made up of invisible and indestructible elements called atoms.

Attica (*adj.* Attic), an area about one thousand square miles, of which Athens is the capital.

Augustus, honorific title given by the Roman senate to Octavian (*Aeneid*).

Bacchae, female worshipers of Dionysus (Bacchus) and title of tragedy by Euripides. See also *Maenads* and *Bacchant[e]*.

Bacchant[e], female follower of Dionysus (Bacchus). See also *Bacchae* and *Maenads*.

Bacchus, see *Dionysus*.

Barbarian, word used by Greeks for non-Greeks, usually without a bad connotation.

Bellerophontes, grandfather of Glaukos (*Iliad*).

Boule, Athenian Council.

Briseis, concubine of Achilleus, taken by Agamemnon (*Iliad*).

Cacus, fire-breathing monster killed by Hercules (*Aeneid*).

Cadmus, grandfather of Pentheus (*Bacchae*).

Caesar, Gaius Julius Caesar, Roman politician who was assassinated in 44 B.C.; also, name taken by Octavian when he was adopted by Caesar according to the terms of the dictator's will (*Aeneid*).

Cephalus, Athenian at whose house the conversation in the *Republic* takes place.

Chaerephon, associate of Socrates (*Clouds* and *Apology*).

Character, a personage in a literary work or the personal traits that make such a personage a well-defined individual.

Charon, ferryman of the dead across the river Styx (*Aeneid*).

Chorus, a group of singers and dancers in Greek drama.

Chryses, priest who unsuccessfully tries to ransom his daughter, Chryseis, from Agamemnon (*Iliad*).

City Dionysia, Athenian festival in honor of Dionysus at which tragedies and comedies were performed.

Cleon, Athenian politician who opposed Diodotus in the Mytilenian Debate (Thucydides).

Cleopatra, Greek queen of Egypt, who, with Antony, was defeated in the battle of Actium by Octavian (*Aeneid*).

Corcyra, island off the western coast of Greece that was involved in the beginning of the Peloponnesian War and on which civil strife between democrats and oligarchs took place (Thucydides).

Coryphaeus (sometimes spelled *Koryphaeus*), leader of the chorus.

Creon, brother-in-law of Oedipus (*Oedipus the King*) and king of Thebes (*Antigone*); also, name of king of Corinth and prospective father-in-law of Jason (*Medea*).

Creusa, wife of Aeneas, who was killed during the destruction of Troy (*Aeneid*).

Cumae, Greek colony in southern Italy in which was located the temple of Apollo visited by Aeneas (*Aeneid*).

Dactylic hexameter, the meter of epic poetry.

Danaans, see *Achaians*.

Deiphobus, brother of Hektor, who married Helen after Paris' death (*Iliad* and *Aeneid*).

Delian League, Greek confederacy led by Athens and formed as offensive and defensive pact against Persia (*Thucydides*).

Delphic oracle, shrine at Delphi, where the Pythia (Apollo's priestess) gave advice and prophecies to visitors (*Oedipus the King* and *Apology*).

Demagogue, leader of the people, but more specifically, a politician who seeks power by appealing to the passions and prejudices of the people.

Democracy, rule of the people.

Democritus of Abdera, pre-Socratic philosopher who, with his teacher Leucippus, developed the atomic theory (see *Atomism*).

Deus ex machina, "god from the machine," used to refer to a divinity who appears at the end of a tragedy to provide a solution for the plot and/or to prophesy what will happen to the characters; also employed in a pejorative sense in modern literary criticism to refer to an improbable character or turn of events introduced by an author to resolve a difficult situation (see *Mechane*).

Dialectic, the process that begins with testing of hypotheses through question and answer (see *Socratic method*) and ends with an understanding of the true nature of justice and, ultimately, of the non-hypothetical first principle, the Good (*Republic*).

Didactic poetry, poetry that gives instruction on a given topic (*On the Nature of the Universe*).

Dido, queen of Carthage and tragic heroine of the *Aeneid*.

Diodotus, Athenian politician, opponent of Cleon in the Mytilenian Debate (*Thucydides*).

Diomedes, Greek warrior who meets, but does not fight, Glaukos (*Iliad*).

Dionysus, god of nature and the theater; central character in *Bacchae*. Also called Bacchus.

Discovery, see *Anagnorisis*.

Drama, a literary work that presents a story by means of dialogue and action.

Dramatic date, the time when the action described in a literary work is supposed to have taken place, as opposed to the actual date of composition.

Dramatic irony, a form of irony according to which literary characters, in word or deed, make assumptions that the reader or audience know to be false, or say things that the characters cannot know the significance of until later in the work.

Ekklesia, Athenian assembly.

Ekkyklema, a platform rolled out on wheels through one of the doors of the skene, on which a tableau was displayed representing the result of an action that had taken place indoors and therefore was unseen by the audience.

Elenchus, see *Socratic method.*

Empiricism, the view that experience, particularly that of the senses, is our only source of knowledge.

Epic, a long poem that tells a story involving gods, heroes, and heroic exploits.

Epicureanism, the philosophy of Epicurus that rejected the involvement of the gods in human life and urged the avoidance of pain.

Epicurus, Hellenistic Athenian philosopher and founder of Epicureanism (*On the Nature of the Universe*).

Episode, scene of dialogue in tragedy.

Epithet, a descriptive word or phrase that is linked with the name of a person or thing.

Error in judgement, see *Hamartia.*

Euripides, Athenian tragic playwright.

Evander, Greek king who came to Italy and settled on the Palatine Hill at the site of Rome; ally of Aeneas (*Aeneid*).

Exodos, exit scene; final scene of a tragedy, following the last choral song.

Exposition, an introduction to the main characters and explanation of the situation that forms the background of the story.

Foil, a person or thing that emphasizes by contrast the distinctive traits of another person or thing.

Foreshadowing, the literary device whereby the author gives hints about what is going to happen later in the story.

Formula, stock phrase, line, or passage characteristic of oral poetry (*Iliad*).

Furor, "violent madness, frenzy"; characteristic displayed by such opponents of Aeneas as Juno, Dido, and Turnus, and sometimes by Aeneas himself (*Aeneid*).

Genre, category of literature in accordance with characteristic form and content.

Glaukon, brother of Plato and one of the interlocutors of the *Republic.*

Glaukos, Trojan ally who meets, but does not fight, Diomedes (*Iliad*).

Haimon (also spelled *Haemon*), son of Creon and fiancé of Antigone (*Antigone*).

Hamartia, "error in judgement"; according to Aristotle's *Poetics*, the cause of the tragic hero's misfortune.

Hekabe, wife of Priam and mother of Hektor (*Iliad*).

Hektor, chief hero of the Trojans (*Iliad*).

Helen, wife of Menelaos, whose abduction by Paris caused the Trojan War (*Iliad*).

Helenos, brother of Hektor, who has prophetic ability (*Iliad*).

Hellenes, name that the Greeks used for themselves (Thucydides).

Hellenistic, name that modern scholars have given to the period of Greek history and culture from the death of Alexander the Great (323 B.C.) to the beginning of the Roman domination of Greece (146 B.C.).

Hephaistos, god who makes peace between Zeus and Hera and also makes armor for Achilleus (*Iliad*).

Hera, sister and wife of Zeus, who favored Achilleus and the Achaians, and hated the Trojans (*Iliad*).

Hercules (Latin spelling; in Greek, *Heracles*), Greek hero and god who kills the monster Cacus; also, a prototype of Aeneas and Augustus (*Aeneid*).

Hermes (also called Argeiphontes), god who escorts Priam to the hut of Achilleus (*Iliad*).

Herodotus, historian of the Persian Wars.

Heroic code, unwritten rules that guide the conduct of the Homeric heroes.

Hesiod, epic poet, contemporary with Homer; composed *Works and Days* and *Theogony*.

Homer, epic poet, author of the *Iliad* and *Odyssey*.

Hubris (also spelled *hybris*), "arrogant pride".

Image, a word picture.

Imagery, the employment of images in a given passage of a literary work, a whole work, or a group of works.

In medias res, "into the middle of things"; a literary device, particulary characteristic of epic, whereby the author begins his narrative in the middle of an action, without exposition.

Ionia, central portion of the coast of Asia Minor and the islands off the coast inhabited by Greeks.

Iris, messenger goddess in the *Iliad*.

Irony, see *Dramatic irony* and *Socratic irony*.

Ismene, sister of the heroine in the *Antigone*.

Iulus, see *Ascanius*.

Jason, hero of the Golden Fleece adventure and husband of Medea (*Medea*).

Jocasta, mother and wife of Oedipus (*Oedipus the King*).

Juno, wife and sister of Jupiter (*Aeneid*); in Latin poetry, identified with Hera.

Jupiter, king of the gods, husband and brother of Juno (*Aeneid*); in Latin poetry, identified with Zeus.

Juturna, sister of Turnus (*Aeneid*).

Kalchas, Greek prophet who explains the cause of the plague in the Achaian camp (*Iliad*).

Kommos, song of lament in tragedy.

Koryphaeus, see *Coryphaeus*.

Latinus, king of Latins (*Aeneid*).

Lenaea, one of Athenian Dionysiac festivals at which comedy was performed.

Leucippus, creator of atomism.

Literary Epic, an epic composed with the aid of writing.

Logographers, term used by Thucydides to refer to the prose writers who came before and were contemporary with Herodotus.

Lucretius, Roman poet and author of *On the Nature of the Universe*, a didactic epic expounding the philosophy of Epicureanism.

Lysistrata, comic heroine of the *Lysistrata*.

Macedonians, a Greek people who inhabited the northernmost part of the Greek mainland and whose blood lines were mixed with non-Greek peoples.

Maenads, female worshipers of Dionysus. See *Bacchae*.

Marathon, plain in Attica where the Athenians defeated the Persians (490 B.C.).

Marcellus, nephew and designated heir of Augustus who died young and appears in the underworld in the *Aeneid*.

Mechane, in Greek theater, a crane, to which a cable with a harness for an actor was attached when the plot required a character (for example, a divinity) to fly; see *Deus ex machina*.

Medea, sorceress heroine of the *Medea*.

Meleagros, Greek hero who, when angered by his mother, withdrew from battle; used as an example in Phoinix's speech to Achilleus in the *Iliad*.

Meletus, one of Socrates' accusers in the *Apology*.

Melos, island that rejected the invitation of Athens to join the Delian League and whose men were put to death and women and children were enslaved by the Athenians (Thucydides).

Memmius, patron of Lucretius to whom *On the Nature of the Universe* is dedicated.

Menelaos, brother of Agamemnon and husband of Helen whom she deserts for Paris. He duels with Paris for Helen as the prize (*Iliad*).

Mercury, messenger god in *Aeneid*, identified with Hermes in Latin poetry.

Metaphor, a comparison without the use of *as* or *like*.

Meter, rhythmical pattern of verse.

Mount Olympos, mountain in northern Greece, home of the gods (*Iliad*).

Muses, goddesses of literature and the arts in general.

Myrmidons, the men of Achilleus (*Iliad*).

Mytilene, city on the island of Lesbos that attempted to revolt from Athens and whose fate is debated by Cleon and Diodotus (Thucydides).

Narrative, a story that presents a series of related actions.

Nestor, aged adviser in the *Iliad*.

New Comedy, a nonpolitical, chorusless form of comedy popular in Athens in the Hellenistic era, characterized by interest in various character types and family relationships.

Niobe, legendary tragic queen used as an example by Achilleus (*Iliad*) and also by Antigone (*Antigone*).

Nomos, any custom or law created by man.

Octavian, grandnephew and adopted son of Julius Caesar who became the first Roman emperor; praised by Vergil as the savior of Rome (*Aeneid*). See *Augustus*.

Odysseus, Achaian hero, member of the embassy to Achilleus (*Iliad*) and hero of the *Odyssey*.

Oedipus, Theban king who unknowingly killed his father and married his mother (*Oedipus the King*).

Oikos, "household."

Old Comedy, form of comedy popular at Athens during the fifth century B.C.; characterized by the prominence of the chorus and political and social satire.

Oligarchy, rule of the few (Thucydides).

Optimates, Roman aristocrats who were defenders of senatorial authority.

Oral poetry, poetry composed by improvisational techniques, involving stock phrases, lines, and passages called formulas (for example, *Iliad* and *Odyssey*).

Orchestra, circular dancing area for the chorus in the Greek theater.

Oxymoron, figure of speech that joins two contradictory terms for paradoxical effect, as in "a wise fool." The word itself is a combination of two Greek words meaning "sharp-dull."

Palatine Hill, one of the seven hills of Rome; the home of Evander and Pallas in the *Aeneid*.

Pallas, son of Evander, whose death is avenged by Aeneas (*Aeneid*).

Parabasis, characterisic feature of Old Comedy. A long choral passage, both recited and sung, representing the views of the poet directly addressed to the audience.

Paris, Hektor's brother, who abducts Helen and thereby causes the Trojan War. Also called Alexandros (*Iliad*).

Parodos, in Greek theater, one of the two gangways that led into the orchestra; also, entrance song of the chorus in tragedy and comedy.

Parody, mimicry of the style of an author or genre in a literary work for the purpose of ridicule.

Patriarchy, father rule.

Patroklos, hero whose death Achilleus avenges when he kills Hektor (*Iliad*).

Patronymic, a name inherited from a paternal ancestor.

Penthesilea, Amazon queen killed by Achilleus at Troy (*Aeneid*).

Pentheus, Theban king, tragic hero of the *Bacchae*.

Peripety, the change from happiness to misery, or vice-versa, experienced by the tragic protagonist according to Aristotle's *Poetics*; also called reversal of fortune.

Personification, figure of speech whereby inanimate objects and abstract ideas are given human qualities and/or form.

Pheidippides, son of Strepsiades in the *Clouds*.

Phenomenalism, the belief that we can only know ideas present in our mind, not objects outside our mind.

Philosophical dialogue, see *Socratic dialogue*.

Philosophy, love of wisdom.

Phoinix, foster father of Achilleus (*Iliad*).

Physis, "nature."

Plato, Athenian philosopher and author of the *Apology* and the *Republic*.

Poetics, work by Aristotle that examines, among other things, the nature of tragedy.

Polemarchus, one of the interlocutors of the *Republic*.

Polis, "city-state."

Polytheism, belief in many gods.

Pompey, Roman general and champion of the Senate who was defeated by Julius Caesar (*Aeneid*).

Populares, Roman aristocrats who presented themselves as champions of the people.

Pre-Socratics, Greek philosophers, of whom some preceded, and others were contemporary with, Socrates.

Priam, king of Troy and father of Hektor (*Iliad* and *Aeneid*).

Primary epic, see *Primitive Epic*.

Primitive epic, epic composed by means of oral techniques of composition.

Prologue, opening scene of dialogue in tragedy and comedy.

Protagonist, the actor in tragedy who took the leading role; also, in modern literary criticism, applied to the central character in a drama or another genre.

Protagoras, leading Sophist who said, "Man is the measure of all things."

Recognition, see *Anagnorisis*.

Reductio ad absurdum, technique of argument that disproves a hypothesis by pointing out the absurdity of its logical conclusion (*Republic*).

Relativism, the view that truth has no independent absolute existence, but is dependent upon the individual and his particular situation.

Reversal of fortune, see *Peripety*.

Rhetoric, the art of persuasion.

Romulus, legendary founder of Rome (*Aeneid*).

Salamis, an island off the coast of which the Greeks defeated the Persians (480 B.C.).

Sarpedon, Lykian hero and ally of the Trojans who was killed by Patroklos (*Iliad*).

Secondary epic, see *Literary epic*.

Sibyl, Apollo's priestess at Cumae who guides Aeneas through the underworld (*Aeneid*).

Simile, comparison introduced by *as* or *like*.

Sinon, Greek spy who tricks the Trojans into bringing the Trojan Horse within their city walls (*Aeneid*).

Skene, stage-building in Greek theater that usually represents a palace, temple, or house.

Skepticism, a doubting state of mind, favored by the Sophists.

Social contract, agreement among members of society neither to do nor to suffer wrong (*Republic* and *On the Nature of the Universe*).

Socrates, Athenian philosopher and central figure of Plato's *Apology* and *Dialogues*.

Socratic dialogue, philosophic conversation involving Socrates as a central interlocutor, used by Plato for philosophical investigation.

Socratic irony, the feigned ignorance of the philosopher.

Socratic method, technique used by Socrates for testing hypotheses by argument and questioning; also called elenchus.

Sophists, professional traveling teachers of rhetoric and other subjects.

Sophocles, Athenian tragedian.

Stasimon, choral song in tragedy.

Stoicism, Hellenistic philosophy that advocated the complete control of one's passions and asserted that everything happens for the best.

Strepsiades, comic hero of the *Clouds*.

Suppliancy, the act of making a humble request; a ritual act, in which the suppliant, while sitting or kneeling, grasps the knees of the person supplicated and touches his chin or kisses his hands. This act of self-humiliation was an attempt to forestall any unfavorable reaction, on the part of the supplicated, to a request.

Teiresias, aged, blind Theban prophet (*Antigone*, *Oedipus the King*, and *Bacchae*).

Theme, a central idea that gives a literary work unity.

Thermopylae, mountain pass in northern Greece in defense of which 300 Spartans were killed by the Persians (480 B.C.).

The Thirty, a committee of Athenian oligarchs who, when given control of Athens in order to revise the constitution, used their power to rid Athens of their democratic enemies (*Apology*).

Thetis, divine mother of Achilleus (*Iliad*).

Thrasymachus, Sophist, one of the interlocutors of the *Republic*.

Thucydides, historian of the Peloponnesian War.

Tiber, river that runs through Rome; also, god of same river (*Aeneid*).

Tragedy, primarily used for a dramatic work, that is, a play in which a central character, called a tragic protagonist or hero, suffers some serious misfortune that is not accidental, and therefore meaningless, but is significant in that the misfortune is logically connected with the hero's actions; also, any significant misfortune suffered by a character in a dramatic or nondramatic work.

Trojans, people led by Hektor against the Greeks in the Trojan War (*Iliad*) and led by Aeneas to Italy (*Aeneid*).

Turnus, Rutulian prince, opponent of Aeneas (*Aeneid*).

Venus, divine mother of Aeneas; in Latin poetry, identified with Aphrodite (*Aeneid*).

Vergil, Roman poet, author of the *Aeneid*.

Vulcan, god who made armor for Aeneas (*Aeneid*); in Latin poetry, identified with Hephaistos.

Zeus, king of gods; brother and husband of Hera (*Iliad*).

Bull. The constellation Taurus the Bull commemorates the form Zeus takes when he carries off Europa to Crete.
Ami-(Asi-), c. 550–530 B.C.